EXPLORIN
THE DORSET COAST PATH

Leigh Hatts

COUNTRYSIDE BOOKS
NEWBURY, BERKSHIRE

First published 1993
© Leigh Hatts 1993

COUNTRYSIDE BOOKS
3 Catherine Road
Newbury, Berkshire

ISBN 1 85306 224 3

Maps and illustrations by Ken Hatts
Cover Photograph of the Golden Cap, Chideock
taken by Andy Williams

Typeset by Acorn Bookwork, Salisbury, Wilts.
Produced through MRM Associates Ltd., Reading
Printed in Great Britain

Contents

Coast Path distances between walks

1 8 miles from Seatown to West Bexington
2 17 miles from Abbotsbury to Redcliff Point
3 3½ miles from Osmington Mills to West Bottom
4 3½ miles from Lulworth to Rings Hill
5 2 miles from Gad Cliff to Kimmeridge Bay
6 1 mile from Hounds-tout to just before the Memorial area above Chapman's Pool
7 2 miles from St Aldhelms Head to Seacombe Bottom
8 2½ miles from Swanage to Ballard Down
9 5 miles from Studland to Branksome Chine
10 4 miles from Bournemouth to Southbourne
11 2 miles from Hengistbury Head to Highcliffe Castle
12 2 miles from Chewton Bunny to Becton Bunny
13 –

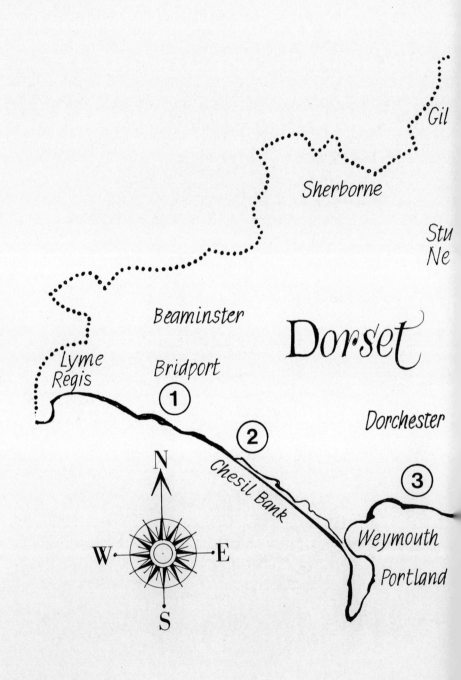

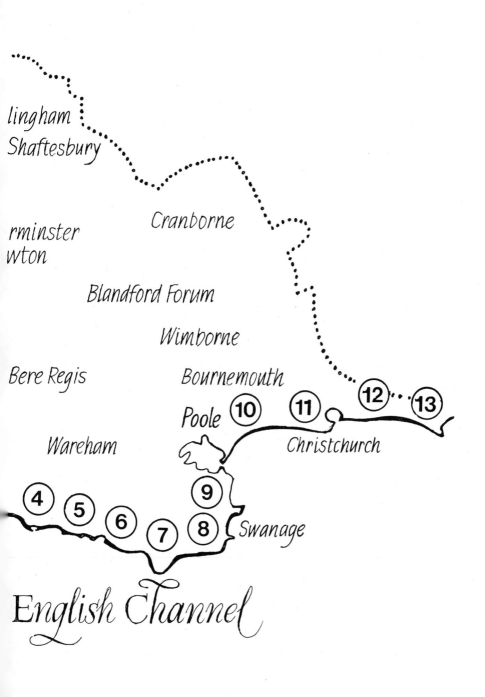

Introduction

The Dorset Coast Path is the 76 mile climax to the 572 mile South West Peninsula Coast Path which starts near Minehead in Somerset. The official end of the coast path is the Poole Harbour entrance but the Dorset climax must be Ballard Down where you not only see the final mile of beach walk below but also the bays of Studland, Poole and Christchurch which lie beyond.

Since 1985 the unofficial Bournemouth Coast Path has continued the coast walk for another 20 miles to the new Dorset border at Chewton Bunny and the beginning of the next official coast path, The Solent Way, at nearby Milford-on-Sea. This book will take the walker on to the Hampshire border and help in the exploration of the best areas in 'new Dorset'.

By chance this eastern end of Dorset shares the characteristics of the west. Both have abandoned ancient churches close to crumbling cliffs which have helped to drive villages further inland. Only the smugglers stayed on. In between are the high chalk cliffs of the Isle of Purbeck. Dorset offers a very wide choice of terrain, for where there is no cliff there may be shingle, sand and occasionally promenade.

The number of Ordnance Survey trig points on these walks is confirmation that the best viewpoints have been included. These solid tripod pillars for measuring angles and distances may be redundant but they remain useful landmarks on hilltops.

If walking on high paths is to be enjoyable, common sense must prevail. You should never go near the cliff edge. Only last year the crumbling Kimmeridge cliff claimed the life of a local villager who thought he knew his own area well. Every year more than one person goes over the cliff somewhere in Dorset and not all survive. Wandering off the well waymarked paths in the Lulworth and Tyneham Army ranges can lead to injury if you touch a shell. But wherever you walk you should observe the Country Code:

Guard against all risks of fire
Fasten all gates
Keep dogs under proper control
Keep to paths across farmland
Avoid damaging fences, hedges and walls
Leave no litter – take it home
Protect wild life, wild plants and trees
Go carefully on country roads
Respect the life of the countryside
Safeguard water supplies

By obeying a few rules your day will usually be very rewarding for many of the views on these walks can only be enjoyed on foot.

Where possible a day's walking will be greatly enhanced by using public transport. Obviously this is easier in Bournemouth than Tyneham which has no bus. But even the Highcliffe walk is well served by trains and it can be an important part of the day to be able to rely on someone else driving after an exhilarating walk. It is also better for the countryside if traffic is reduced. On the Isle of Purbeck in the summer it is an advantage to use the bus from Bournemouth as it has priority over all other vehicles on the toll road from Poole Harbour.

The whole of the Dorset Coast Path is incorporated into this book and if you are doing the full walk the relevant sections are clearly indicated in each chapter. For those who prefer to sample the delights of the Dorset coast in smaller doses, anything from 4 to 10 miles, I have arranged the book as a series of circular walks, taking in sections of the Coast Path and the countryside inland.

Sketch maps are supplied for each walk but the relevant Ordnance survey map in the Pathfinder and Outdoor Leisure series is noted, should you wish to follow the route in more detail. Each walk includes a section of historical notes on points of interest along the way.

Leigh Hatts
Spring 1993

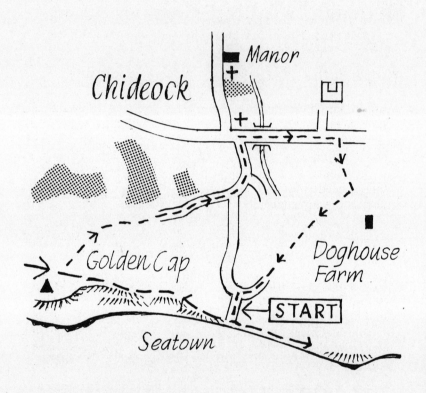

Seatown, Golden Cap and Chideock

(Coast Path – Seatown to West Bexington)

Introduction: Chideock is in a corner of Dorset remote enough to have been able to keep the 'Old Faith' alive in penal times and maintain a smuggling community down by the shore. Both interests would have found Golden Cap, the highest point on the south coast, a useful lookout. The walk is short but plenty of time is needed for the very steep climb, enjoying the view and exploring the unusual village.

Distance: A 4 mile circular route which includes a mile long climb up the Golden Cap cliff. Map: OS Pathfinder 1317.

Refreshments: The Anchor Inn at Seatown is open until 2pm and from 7pm daily, but all day in summer when cream teas are available. In Chideock there are two thatched pubs, The Clock (opposite St Giles) and The George (at the eastern end of the village). Betchworth House Hotel (west of St Giles) serves cream teas as well as welcoming walkers for bed and breakfast.

How to get there: Chideock is on the A35 between Lyme Regis and Bridport. The Seatown turning is signposted opposite the church. Southern National bus X31 runs between Dorchester BR station and Axminster BR station (0305 783645 for details). As the bus stops in Chideock passengers may prefer to start the walk in the village rather than at Seatown where the car park is located.

Coast Path: From Seatown turn eastwards up Ridge Cliff. Keep on the cliff top to descend to Eype Mouth. Cross the stepping stones and climb up West Cliff. The path runs inland of limestone workings before running down to Bridport Harbour. On the far side follow the steep path to the cliff top. Later there is a short diversion to cross the river Bride. The path twice drops down to beaches at Burton and Cogden. From here the stony beach (Chesil Bank) is the path to West Bexington (see Walk Two).

The Walk: Start at Seatown outside the Anchor Inn. Walk down to the sea and turn right to follow a path which begins at the side of the toilets and winds up the cliff to a flight of steps. Follow the grassy clifftop path which continues to gain height before the view is lost behind bushes. Where the path divides keep left to find a wooden stile.

Follow the path, which can be seen running across grass past a wind bent tree, to climb up to an east facing seat near the top of Golden Cap. At the side of the seat go over a double stile and uphill with a fence to a stile (left).

Only to enjoy the view from Golden Cap, go over the stile and follow the path up to the OS trig point on the summit.

The walk continues to the right of the stile down to a double stile by a gate – this is the direct continuation of the path from the summit. Go over a field and through a gateway to follow a lane running ahead alongside Langdon Hill wood (left). To the right there is a view down to the valley.

Soon the lane begins to run downhill. After a gateway another lane joins from the left. At a fork go left down the narrower (and often muddy) branch. This is Pettycrate Lane which at a house gains a metalled surface. At a junction in Chideock go left along Duck Street (a continuation of Sea Hill Lane). Pass Mill Lane and the thatched Swiss Cottage (right) to reach the main road by St Giles church.

The walk continues to the right down the main road and over the tiny river Winniford. Continue past Ruins Lane (left) and The George. On reaching a red telephone box turn right down a narrow path.

Beyond a stile continue ahead along the side of a field (right). Cross a footbridge and a stile to bear half left across the next field. Go over a stile by a gate, cross an approach to Doghouse Farm and follow an enclosed footpath running half right. At the end the path goes through a kissing gate and follows a fence round a bend.

At a lane keep ahead to cross the tiny river Winniford again. Immediately go through the kissing gate on the left and bear half right over the field. Continue across a track to another kissing gate and walk over the grass. Turn left along a narrow concrete road running between caravan parks. At the shop follow the main road ahead to the Seatown seafront.

Historical Notes

Seatown should not be confused with Seaton beyond the county boundary to the west. Seatown was never a town although the hamlet was once larger. In the 18th century at least 30 families lived here engaged in fishing and smuggling. The Chideock Gang of smugglers was led by 'The Colonel' whose identity has never been revealed. But they were well organised using packhorses and selling goods in Somerset and even further north. Since those days the cliffs have crumbled taking away a road up to Golden Cap and house to the south of the pub. In 1685 the Monmouth Rebellion was quickly ended at the Battle of Sedgemoor thanks to a customs officer who reported a landing here by three men from a ship which was putting ashore troops at Lyme Regis. Seatown's shop opens in the summer when the population expands with use of the caravan site.

Golden Cap takes its name from the orange sandstone and golden gorse around the summit. This cliff, the highest on the south coast, is 626 ft high and on a clear day affords a view east to Portland and west to the Devon coast beyond Lyme Regis. Looking down into the valley to the north west can be seen the ruined chapel of St Gabriel. This and the next door farmhouse are the remains of the village of Stanton St Gabriel which once had a main coast road running through. The church was replaced in 1841 by another St Gabriel's at Morcomelake a mile to the north, where the Norman font can be found. On the viewpoint is not only an Ordnance Survey trig point but also a memorial to Lord Antrim, chairman of the National Trust which has owned this landmark since 1974.

Chideock, pronounced 'Chiddick', is unusual for a village in having two historic churches. The oldest is Anglican St Giles's which has a 13th century nave and the 15th century Arundell Chapel containing a black marble tomb figure of Sir John Arundell who died in 1545. The Roman Catholic church of Our Lady and St Ignatius, attached to the manor house ½ mile up the lane at the side of St Giles, incorporates a barn where mass was said secretly during penal times for the Arundell family who maintained the 'Old Faith'. In 1802 the property was bought by a cousin, Thomas Weld (see page 37), who gave it to his son Humphrey Weld. It was his artistic son Charles who transformed the building into the present Romanesque style church and worked on the wall paintings himself.

Humphrey, brother of Cardinal Weld, built the present manor house which is still occupied by the family. However, in 1987 it became the Duke and Duchess of York's temporary home whilst Prince Andrew was stationed at Portland Naval Base. The house contains the village museum (entry via the church 10am to 4pm except Sunday mornings – free).

The Arundells lived on the manor house site only after Chideock Castle had been destroyed in 1645 by Roundhead forces who bombarded it from three sides. The return fire hit St Giles's tower. Although the gatehouse still existed in 1733, all the stone has now disappeared and the castle site, at the end of Ruins Lane, is marked by a cross commemorating the Chideock Martyrs. In 1594 Lady Arundell's chaplain John Cornelius, two of her servants John Carey and Patrick Salmon and a relative, Thomas Bosgrave, were arrested for Catholic activity and executed. Fifty years later a successor chaplain, Hugh Green, was sentenced to death for being a Catholic priest. The two priests and Thomas Bosgrave have been declared to be 'Blessed' by the Pope.

Thomas Daniel, the Arundells' steward who helped defend the castle, is buried outside St Giles's east window. Now the Catholic burial ground is on the north side of the churchyard where the Weld Mausoleum stands.

Abbotsbury, West Bexington and Abbotsbury Castle

(Coast Path – West Bexington to Redcliff Point)

Introduction: Although this is a circular walk almost all the route stays on the coast path. Long distance walkers can stay by the coast on the official path or take an alternative official coast path which runs along the top of the South Dorset Ridgeway. This inland path not only offers wide views but is a more natural route for a traveller. By using the two paths for this round walk it is possible to embrace both the coast path where Lawrence of Arabia used to ride his famous motorcycle at high speed and the castle site offering the best view of the village with its 600 year old swannery.

Distance: A 7 mile circular route with one long steep climb. Map: OS Pathfinder 1331.

Refreshments: Abbotsbury's Ilchester Arms serves bar meals and welcomes children but for tea the teashops are best. At West Bexington there is a café by the beach open in season and The Manor Hotel serving good bar food including home-made soup and cream teas all year.

How to get there: Abbotsbury is on the B3157 between Bridport and Weymouth. There is no daily public transport (see *Public Transport in Rural Dorset*, free from the county council).

Coast Path: See Introduction (above) for explanation of official paths. Follow this walk from West Bexington. Walkers wishing

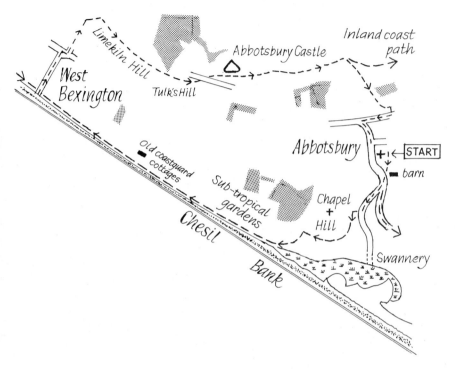

to stay on the coast should continue ahead along Chesil Bank making use of a track just behind the beach. On meeting the end of a road from Abbotsbury continue forward to find the way joining an enclosed lane which runs round the bottom of Chapel Hill to the edge of Abbotsbury.

To continue eastwards take the Tithe Barn road to Horsepool Farm where a path runs steeply up to the top of a ridge. After running high above another farm the path turns south down the side of Hodder's Coppice and east alongside Ansty's Withy Bed. Cross a road to follow the edge of Wyke Woods. At the end turn down its east side to enter a valley. Keep left of buildings ahead and later cross a stream before reaching the coast – protected by Chesil Bank across the water. From here, apart from cutting one corner and avoiding a small army camp, the path is by the shoreline as far as Weymouth.

17

Leave the town by following the sea wall to Overcombe. Here walkers often follow the beach to Bowleaze Cove although the official way is over the cliff. At the Cove pass on the seaward side of The Riviera Hotel to climb up to a stile by a Weymouth borough boundary stone. Ahead is Redcliff Point (see Walk Three).

The Walk: Walk to the church and pass through the church-yard's wooden gate. Walk round to the south side of the church to cross the remains of the abbey church wall and leave the churchyard by the south gateway. Keep ahead on a gravelled path past a remaining cloister building (left) down to the pond in front of the great barn. Bear right to rejoin the road.

Turn left to pass the barn entrance but where the lane divides take the right fork. After a short distance go over a stone stile on the right. The path bends round to the right to a wooden stile. Bear right and after crossing a stream turn left along the side of a bank to a path which runs round the base of Chapel Hill. St Catherine's chapel can be seen up to the right. The path runs south past a wooden waymark to enter a wood at a stile.

The path later bears round to the right to a wooden stile. Here there is a view down onto the Swannery by Chesil Bank. There is soon a stone marker and then a wartime pill box (left). Later the path is beside a fence (left) and ahead can be seen the trees of the Sub-tropical Gardens. The path runs downhill to a wooden stile by a lane.

Turn left along the lane which bears west and after a gate joins the beach – part of Chesil Bank. The path runs along the back of the beach. Where the road from the village meets the beach there is a duckboard walk up to the top of the stones.

Here, beyond a gate, the coast path continues along the metalled access road behind the beach. Soon the road is above the beach with good views. The hard surface continues for a mile to the weatherboarded coastguard cottages on the boundary of Abbotsbury parish. After the flagstaff at Greenbanks, the way is increasingly rough until it is running over beach stones in front of the wooden holiday chalets at West Bexington.

Turn up the road which beyond the café runs steeply uphill. Just beyond The Manor Hotel (right) there is a junction. Go ahead up the rough lane signposted 'Hardy Monument'. The hedged way climbs steeply. After ¼ mile take the right fork which runs up to within a few yards of the Bridport-Abbotsbury road.

A stile by a gate leads onto the top of Limekiln Hill where there is a National Trust sign. Later an arrow on a wooden post indicates that the path veers slightly to the right towards a further post in the gorse. Beyond here a stone stile carries the way on to the approach to Tulk's Hill.

After 400 yards the path begins to run down to Labour-in-Vain Farm. Here bear leftwards uphill to a signpost near the road. Continue parallel to the road and over the top of Tulk's Hill. At a stile by the road cross over to a gate opposite.

The path continues in an easterly direction parallel with the road. Soon the way climbs to run along the top of the Abbotsbury Castle hill. Beyond the Ordnance Survey trig point head for the beacon. Cross the metalled lane below and go over the stile. The way continues ahead with a view of the Hardy Monument.

Keep along Wears Hill with a view of Wears Farm immediately inland and Chapel Hill to the right. The ground is open but later the way is by a fence (left). After a wooden stile bear half right (there is a signpost ahead) away from the main ridge path to begin the descent down into Abbotsbury.

The path soon runs past an amphitheatre down to a gate by a barn. Continue to another gate and bear half left along a ledge path which beyond a gate becomes an enclosed lane. After a double bend the lane reaches the village. Go right for the Ilchester Arms and the village centre.

Historical Notes

Abbotsbury means 'Abbots town'. The Benedictine monastery was founded about 1026 by King Knut's steward. There is a Purbeck marble effigy of an early abbot in the church porch. From at least 1393 the monks maintained a swannery just behind Chesil Bank to supplement the refectory table. The

19

swannery survived the monastery's closure in 1539 by Henry VIII to become today's leading swan conservation centre. Another survival is the magnificent 15th century thatched Tithe Barn which is a country museum. (The Swannery and Barn are open daily but in winter on Sundays only; admission charge for adults.) The Abbot had the right to a portion of every fisherman's catch – often mackerel – and to all wrecks on Chesil Bank. The latter claim seems to have continued after the Reformation for in 1752 a London newspaper reported 'All the people of Abbotsbury, including the Vicar, are thieves, smugglers, and plunderers of wrecks'.

The original Abbey House near the church was destroyed when a powder magazine blew up inside during the Civil War. Abbotsbury was Royalist and Cavaliers fired from the 15th century church tower whilst Roundheads left permanent bullet holes in the pulpit. Immediately south of this parish church was the Abbey church of which only a fragment of wall remains in the churchyard. The hilltop St Catherine's Chapel was built as a navigation guide by the monks in the 14th century.

Chesil Bank or Beach runs south east for 11 miles to Portland just below Weymouth. Legend says that the stony beach, which forms a long lagoon with the coast, was washed up in one night. In 1824 the bank was breached by a storm which swept away the village of Fleet leaving only a church ruin. In 1943 it was the location for trial runs with dummy bouncing bombs for the famous Dambusters' Raid. Sea holly grows here and in spring and early summer there is white sea campion, pink thrift and yellow horned poppy.

Sub-tropical Gardens cover 20 acres of woodland in a sheltered valley which allows plants normally found in glasshouses to thrive. Rhododendrons are an attraction in early summer. The gardens were started in the early 19th century by the Earl of Ilchester whose house was eventually pulled down in 1934. (Open daily except winter Mondays; admission charge for adults.)

East Bexington is part of Abbotsbury and its weatherboarded coastguard cottages are on the very edge of the parish. When the last coastguards left in 1926 the building was bought by novelist Henry Major Tomlinson who wrote *Between the Lines* and *All Our Yesterdays* here. In the 1930s he had his own house built nearby which he called Gallions Reach after the book he proof read soon after arriving at the coastguard cottages.

West Bexington: The manor house, mentioned in the Domesday Book, was rebuilt by Sir Robert Napier in the 1680s and became the summer home for the family whose main residence is just over a mile inland at Puncknowle. The seaside house, which has a Jacobean panelled hall, is now The Manor Hotel with a cellar bar and a tearoom. This remains a quiet hamlet despite a plan in the 1930s to turn this former smugglers' community into Bexington-on-Sea.

Limekiln Hill is a former stone working now given over to rough grazing. The restored limekiln is just below the path at the top of the hill which has been owned by the National Trust since 1964.

Abbotsbury Castle is a 10 acre Iron Age hillfort which was probably fortified by the Romans who succeeded the Durotriges tribe which also occupied Maiden Castle near Dorchester.

Hardy Monument was erected in 1844 in memory of Vice-Admiral Sir Thomas Hardy who was present at Nelson's death. The high point had been part of the beacon chain during the Napoleonic period and the present beacon next to the monument links to the one at Abbotsbury Castle. The Hardy Monument can be reached eventually on the inland coast path.

21

Osmington, Redcliff Point and Osmington Mills

(Coast Path – Redcliff Point to West Bottom)

Introduction: Like the Abbotsbury walk most of this circular route is on the coast path as this is where the dual routes come together. From these cliffs, known to artist John Constable, there are the best views of Portland and the sweep of Weymouth Bay. The inland coast path used for this walk's return to the village offers a good aspect of the famous white horse on the hill behind Osmington.

Distance: A 4 mile circular route. Map: OS Pathfinder 1332.

Refreshments: Osmington's Sunray pub has bar meals and welcomes children. The nearby Fermoy Tearooms, by the turning to the church, is open daily and has a reasonably priced menu as well as selling secondhand books. At Osmington Mills there is a tearoom open in season and the Smugglers' Inn, serving bar meals, open until 2.30pm and from 6.30pm daily but all day in summer.

How to get there: Osmington is on the A353 east of Weymouth. There is a bus (Wilts and Dorset X65) on summer Sundays from Bournemouth Pier. (If you wish to check, call 0202 673555.)

Coast Path: Follow this walk from Redcliff Point to Osmington Mills.

The path continues eastwards round the left hand side of the pub. Go up to the top seaward side of the field to follow the

22

cliff top as far as Ringstead. Here the way is inland of buildings to go uphill onto Burning Cliff. Below is a nature reserve. Pass behind a chapel but keep ahead where the main path swings left. After Holworth House gates stay on the cliff top past White Nothe viewpoint to West Bottom where there is a large navigation beacon (see Walk Four).

The Walk: The walk starts at the church lychgate. Walk through the churchyard and up the north side of the church to find a footpath at the far end.

The path leads to a stile. Bear half left across the field to find a gap between the line of back gardens. Go through the gate and turn right on the pavement along the main road to pass School House and Postbox Cottage. After a few yards cross the road to enter a gap opposite.

Keep directly ahead through two gates by a barn (right). Beyond a stile still keep forward by a hedge (left). Soon there is a view of Portland ahead. Go over a stile by a gate and bear half right down the field – there is usually a slight tread.

At the bottom go over a stile and turn right past a signpost. At once go down the raised path to head towards the abandoned stone building below. At the bottom of the slope keep by the hedge (left). On reaching the ruined Ewelease Barn go left over the stile by a gate. Bear up to the right towards the signpost which points to Redcliff Point. As indicated keep in a south westerly direction.

Do not go over the stile (with the Preston signpost) but walk through the gap just below. Keep forward, with the rising Redcliff point over to the left, to the far left corner of the field and join the coast path.

To the right is a stile by a Weymouth boundary stone. But the walk continues to the left up to Redcliff Point. At once there is a view inland of the White Horse. Where the path appears to divide keep left to stay near the fence and climb the hill to the top of Redcliff Point where you can see as far as St Aldhelm's Head in the east. Continue downhill staying near the fence and at the bottom bear left to find a wooden footbridge.

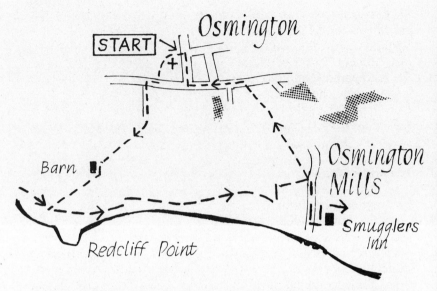

Turn right to follow the grass path along the cliff top. The path narrows and then runs downhill to cross a footbridge just below a holiday camp. The way then climbs and becomes enclosed until reaching a stile at the end of the camp fence.

The path now appears to leave the cliff top by running half left up the hill ahead towards a signpost on the horizon. At the top continue ahead and soon the path runs through blackberry bushes and over two stiles. The path now follows a grassy ledge. There is a pond down to the left before the path descends at steps into a lightly wooded area known as Black Head. A series of long footbridges leads to a wooden stile.

Due to a landslip the path no longer returns to the cliffside but continues eastward on a well waymarked route along the edge (right) of a large field. The way runs down to the corner where there is duckboarding and a wooden stile.

To reach Osmington Mills go right over the stile and down a narrow passage to turn right again at a lane.

To continue the walk back to Osmington village go left along the duckboarding and stay by the hedge (right) up to the far end of the field.

Go over the stile by a gate and go ahead up the field keeping the hill to the left and a telegraph pole to the right. There is a signpost ahead just before a stile which comes into view at the last moment. From here there is a view of the White Horse on the hill behind Osmington. Bear half left down the field towards a house and the church. On the way cross a hidden stile by a gate. From the stile between the dairy and house go ahead to the main road. Cross over to the pavement and turn left to reach the pub and village centre.

Historical Notes

Osmington was 'Osmyntone' to the Saxons but is not derived from the church's dedication to St Osmund who lived later – in the 11th century. The village retains a thatched post office and even the new 1990s houses opposite The Sunray are stone and thatch. The ruins of the 17th century manor are on the north side of the churchyard. Osmington was once the seat of the Warham family which included Archbishop William Warham who crowned Henry VIII. The salmon coloured Old Vicarage was John Constable's honeymoon lodging for about six weeks in the autumn of 1816. The vicar had married the couple at St Martin-in-the-Fields. Constable's many sketches resulted in the 'Weymouth Bay' oil which hangs still incomplete in the National Gallery. His other local paintings show Osmington's cliffs and village.

Osmington church: The tower is 15th century but most of the main building was reconstructed in 1846, incorporating the early 13th century chancel arch. A window on the south side contains ancient glass from war damaged cathedrals, abbeys and churches in Flanders and France. By the altar is a memorial to John Fisher who was vicar when John Constable stayed at the Vicarage. Fisher was the nephew of the Bishop of Salisbury whose friendship resulted in the famous cathedral paintings. Constable's portraits of the vicar and his wife, painted here in 1816, are now in the FitzWilliam Museum at Cambridge.

Osmington Mills has lost the mills but still has its pub dating from the 13th century, complete with a brewery building at the back. The partly thatched Smugglers' Inn has a fireplace where a customs officer hid one summer day in the 1790s hoping to hear smuggler Pierre Latour incriminate himself. But 'French Peter', alerted in code by the landlord (who offered him a drink other than his usual cognac), asked for the fire to be lit claiming that the channel crossing had been unseasonably chilly. The revenue officer was forced to reveal himself. Later the successful Latour married the landlord's daughter and lived in style in France. Then the pub was called The Crown. It had become The Picnic by the 1920s when visitors came for lobster and strawberry teas. The present name, recalling the old days, was adopted as recently as 1973.

Osmington White Horse was carved into the hillside between May and August 1808 to commemorate George III's many holidays in nearby Weymouth. The 320 ft high figure of the King on horseback is a copy in reverse of an equestrian portrait in Weymouth Guildhall. Architect James Hamilton, who was responsible for the famous George III statue in Weymouth erected two years later, designed the White Horse to be dug a little out of proportion to allow for viewing from a distance and at a lower level. The cutting of the outline by 12 army engineers was supervised by a Weymouth bookseller and a mysterious John Ranier privately financed the project. Before the end of the century many myths had become attached to the hillside landmark. One guidebook even suggested that the horse was Saxon with George III added later.

Portland is a bleak island now joined to the mainland by a narrow road. Henry VIII founded the naval base which has only recently been run down. One of the last to be stationed there was Prince Andrew. Portland stone was used by Sir Christopher Wren at St Paul's Cathedral. The famous prison provided labour for the quarry.

Lulworth Cove, Durdle Door, West Bottom and Newlands Farm

(Coast Path – West Bottom to Rings Hill)

Introduction: 'The most beautiful place in England' is how poet Rupert Brooke described Lulworth in 1907. The first stretch of the walk may be quite crowded but most walkers never get beyond Durdle Door and any who do are often defeated by the very steep climb at Scratchy Bottom. This walk has three oddities – a post box too high to reach, modern sculpture on a field boundary and a blue telephone box.

Distance: A 6 mile circular route with several very steep climbs. Map: OS Outdoor Leisure 15 (Purbeck).

Refreshments: The Castle Inn in the village is open until 2.30pm and from 7pm daily. Teas are available from The Mill House Hotel, Bishop's Cottage and the Beach Café which are all near the cove.

How to get there: West Lulworth lies at the end of the B3071, 4 miles south of Wool. Details of the Little Red Bus (which runs between Wool station and Lulworth on certain days) and taxis can be obtained on 0929 462467/463395.

Coast Path: Follow this walk from the west end of West Bottom, but walkers wishing to stay on the coast should walk round the top of West Bottom and continue along the cliff top past Durdle Door to Lulworth Cove. This walk's inland route to Lulworth

27

Cove is easier than the steep rises and falls of the cliff top.

Walkers wishing to continue beyond Lulworth should phone 0929 462721 ext 4819/4859 in advance to check that the Army firing ranges are open to the public. Climb the steps beside the cove café. The path runs round the top of the cove to Little Bindon. The way is well waymarked by the army and stays by the cliff top until climbing Rings Hill above Worbarrow Bay (see Walk Five).

The Walk: The walk starts at the large car park behind the Post Office and Heritage Centre near the sea. Go through the gate at the back and follow the wide path which runs up the side of the hill, Hambury Tout. Beyond a gate and stiles, the path is open and provides a good view back down onto the cove with St Aldhelm's head beyond. Ahead, Portland soon comes into view.

At the top there is a view down onto the Durdle Door promontory with the smaller natural arch at Bat's Head visible beyond. The path runs downhill along the edge of St Oswald's Bay. (Here the footpath is just outside a cliff top fence but

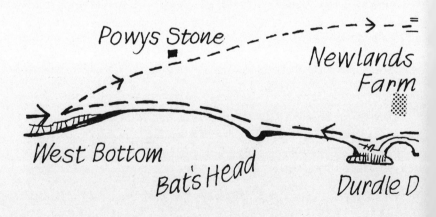

provision has been made for the occasional use of a temporary path inside the fence to allow grass to grow on the definitive path.) There is a stile to cross before the path joins a better used path from the right just before the Durdle Door viewpoint.

The coast path continues westwards by going uphill and then gently down into Scratchy Bottom. The climb up the far side is very steep but the view at the top, known as Swyre Head, includes the triangular navigation beacon near the walk's turning point at West Bottom.

The way is again downhill before the climb up the side of Bat's Head. Walkers should go straight up keeping nearer to the fence (right) than the cliff edge. At the top the path bears to the right to continue in a more gentle climb. At Middle Bottom the way begins to descend on an inland tilt before losing the guiding fence and running up the side of the hill ahead. There are occasional wooden steps made from old signposts.

Near the top, the path is briefly near a cliff drop before curving up towards the navigation beacon. Here there is once more a fence (right). Follow the fence by walking round the

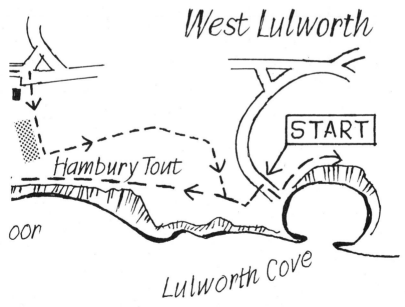

29

curve of West Bottom. On the far side a stone waymark indicates a path to Daggers Gate.

Here leave the coast path and go over the stile by the gate. Stay near the field boundary (left) and soon two paths join from the left. As the field rises the path runs a little away from the fence (left) to cut the field corner ahead – although, as the tread indicates, many walkers hug the fence. Near the field corner (left) there is a stone memorial to Llewelyn Powys.

The path continues eastward along a field boundary (left) where there are surprise shell sculptures in stone alcoves. Over to the left is another navigation beacon and half right can be seen the cliffs. After a gate the way ahead is gently uphill to a fine viewpoint by one of the familiar stone waymarks.

Continue forward downhill and beyond a gateway there is a view (right) down to Bat's Head. On reaching a gate leading to an enclosed track do not go ahead but over the stile to the right. At once bear half right towards a lonely waymark post. At the field corner go through the gap to follow the high bank (left). Down to the right can be seen Scratchy Bottom and across the valley is a caravan site. At a gate go over the stile to follow the enclosed way down to Newlands Farm.

At the farm turn right and follow the farm road round a bend by the farmhouse. Continue to a gateway at a road and at once go right down a grass path at the side of it. Follow the metalled private way through the caravan park. There are shops (open in season) by the blue telephone box.

As soon as the caravans end go left to a stile below Hambury Tout. Once over the stile turn left. There are a couple more stiles as the path runs in the direction of West Lulworth. Just before the path becomes a track go over a stile ahead on the right. The path continues in the same direction before bearing to the right round the hill to meet the outward path. Turn left for the Lulworth Cove car park.

Historical Notes

West Lulworth: The church is surprisingly new, having been opened as recently as 1870 to replace a tiny Norman church whose site is marked by the graveyard near the Castle Inn. The Victorian church was built with Purbeck stone and some materials from the old church. Shipwreck wood was used for part of the reredos. Above a window at the east end can be seen the old inscription 'de Lollworth' from which the village name derives.

The centre of the village is the bus shelter by the Victorian post box preserved high up above a seat. At the start of the lane to the church is Churchfield House which for about a century until 1851 was the Red Lion pub. George III called in for lunch, sometimes without notice, when staying at Weymouth in the 1790s. After the licence finally lapsed in 1886 the old pub was rented out as holiday accommodation. In 1900 social reformers Sidney and Beatrice Webb stayed for three weeks whilst working on one of their books. Sidney read 26 books sent down by the London Library and Beatrice wrote in her diary that she was 'completely satisfied with the companionship and comradeship of my partner, lover, husband' but added 'are the books we have written worth the babies we might have had?' Over the next decade the cottage was often occupied by their fellow Fabian Society member Rupert Brooke.

But in 1910 the poet stayed at the Gothic Cove Cottage opposite the Mill Pond near the sea. The next door Bishop's Cottage teashop was the holiday home of John Wordsworth, Bishop of Salisbury from 1885 to 1911, who added a room as each of his six children was born.

The Lulworth Cove Heritage Centre, next to the post office, is open daily except winter Mondays and Fridays (admission charge).

Lulworth Cove: The cove was once busy with coal being landed for the village and castle (see page 37) and fishermen hanging nets across the entrance. Until 1965 pleasure steamers regularly called from Weymouth – a gangway was wheeled out to the bow. In August 1790 John Carroll, the USA's first Roman Catholic bishop, left here in disguise at dawn having been secretly consecrated bishop in Lulworth Castle's chapel. Just over a decade later Napoleon was believed to have made an undercover night landing – a French speaking smuggler's wife overheard strangers discussing invasion possibilities. In 1820 the poet John Keats stood here on English soil for the last time when his Naples-bound ship made an unexpected call whilst awaiting a favourable wind. It may be offshore that he wrote the sonnet 'Bright star, would I were steadfast as thou art'. Ninety years later Rupert Brooke accidently dropped a book of Keats' poetry overboard from his rowing boat in the cove and had to dive in to retrieve it.

High on the cliff to the west is a redbrick house called Weston built in 1927 for Edward VII's former doctor Sir Alfred Fripp. Architect Edwin Lutyens gave his services free as payment for a medical bill.

Hambury Tout, known locally as Hambury Hill, has a barrow on the top. When opened in 1790 a crouched skeleton was found with a food vessel and ashes.

St Oswald's Bay: Sir John Millais set his painting *Romans leaving Britain* here. The oil, exhibited at the Royal Academy in 1865, shows a Roman legionary saying farewell to his mistress on the cliff at the east end with the view west as the background.

Durdle Door is a Purbeck natural stone arch formed in the sea and known to the Saxons. 'Durdle' is a derivation of the Saxon 'durch' meaning 'through'.

Portland: See Walk Three.

Powys Stone: The ashes of writer Llewelyn Powys (1884–1939) who wrote extensively on Dorset and walked this area were placed here in 1947 by sculptor Elizabeth Muntz – the only woman to be admitted to the Ancient Company of Marblers and Stone Cutters at its annual Shrove Tuesday meeting at Corfe Castle.

Shell sculpture: The three shell-like forms in Purbeck stone, called 'Wayside Carving', are by Peter Randall-Page and were

32

placed in the alcoves in 1988 after being commissioned by Common Ground and the Weld Estate.

Newlands Farm: Philosopher Bertrand Russell often stayed here between 1916 and the mid 1930s. He tended to bring such female friends as Lady Ottoline Morrell, Katherine Mansfield and Colette O'Neill who included Lulworth in a novel about her relationship with Russell. His visitors sometimes shocked villagers by bathing nude in the cove.

Tyneham, Gad Cliff, Worbarrow Bay and Rings Hill

(Coast Path – Rings Hill to Kimmeridge Bay)

Introduction: This walk cannot be attempted every day of the year but those who visit on the many weekends and holiday periods when the Army firing ranges are open will find a place unlike any other along the coast. The village has been uninhabited for half a century leaving a beautiful valley to become an unofficial nature reserve with such birds as the merlin, hobby, buzzard and peregrine falcon all found here. The Army has waymarked the footpaths with yellow posts and these should be strictly followed as anyone straying risks injury from hidden shells.

Distance: A 4 mile circular route which includes two very steep climbs and fantastic views. Map: OS Outdoor Leisure 15 (Purbeck).

Refreshments: None.

How to get there: Tyneham is in a valley south of the Wareham to Lulworth road and to the west of Steeple. There is a car park in the village but no public transport. The village and its approach road are open most weekends, at Christmas holiday time and in August but visitors should check by phoning a Tourist information centre or 0929 462721 ext 4819 or 4859.

Coast Path: Follow this walk from Rings Hill to Gad Cliff but walkers wishing to stay on the coast should turn right (south) to

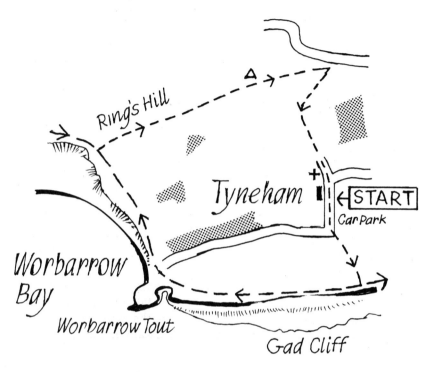

find a stile and follow the well waymarked path down into the bay and up to Gad Cliff.

At Gad Cliff turn left (unless already on the coast path) and at the next path junction go right to zig-zag downhill with the coast. Apart from an obvious short cut at Broad Bench headland, the path stays on the low cliff as far as Kimmeridge Bay where the Army ranges zone ends (see Walk Six).

The Walk: At Tyneham village car park turn away from the buildings and walk through the gateway to the south to reach a T junction beyond the trees. Cross the stile ahead and bear half left up the field on a path lined with yellow posts. On the far side the grass way turns right to go steeply uphill towards a stile on the horizon.

At the top continue ahead to a T junction and turn right

35

along Gad Cliff. The way is sheltered from the sea by the rising bank which should not be climbed. Half right ahead is a view across Worbarrow Bay. On crossing a stile there is a first chance to look back and see Kimmeridge's Clavell Tower and St Aldhelm's Head. The path becomes fenced and ahead can be seen Weymouth Bay. The way runs gently downhill on Gold Down before coming to a viewpoint for the entire bay. Ahead there is a brief view of the Lulworth Army Camp.

Follow the steep fenced path downhill to a stile at the end of the bay behind Worbarrow Tout. Keep ahead past the village track, down a few steps and left down a rough path. Just before the beach go right past the remains of a building, over a foot-bridge and uphill with the yellow waymarks.

The path follows a fence (left) but shortly beyond a wooden stile the waymarks lead the path away from the cliff edge and straight up the very steep Rings Hill ahead. At the top there is a stile.

Continue ahead for a few yards to a stone waymark. Directly ahead is a view down onto Lulworth Castle and church. Turn right on a path which at first is sheltered with good views to the north. At a gate there is a view half right of St Aldhelm's Head. Soon a path joins from the left and the way rises to an Ordnance Survey trig point on Whiteway Hill. Here there is a view across to Poole and beyond the woodland below can be seen Wareham's church tower.

The path runs downhill to a stile at a gateway. After a few yards bear right with the rough crosstrack to walk down the side of the valley to Tyneham. A stile and gate lead to the main street. Turn left for the car park.

Historical Notes

Tyneham: The entire village was 'temporarily' evacuated just before Christmas 1943 so that the area could be used for the army's tank practice. The inhabitants left a message pinned to the church door: 'Please treat the church and houses with care. We have given up our homes, where many of us have lived for generations, to help win the war and keep men free. We shall return one day and thank you for treating the village kindly'.

Despite protests the village remains deserted and part of a firing range but access is now allowed more regularly. One resident returned to find that the pot plant she had given to the postmistress had become a tree. The telephone box is a 1920's 'Kiosk No 1' which pre-dates the famous red 'K2'. The manor house was pulled down but the cottages have recently been made safe and the deconsecrated church has an exhibition about Tyneham. When in 1975 range warden and former stone-mason Roy Cobb cleaned and repaired the churchyard's tombs he found the oldest to be dated 1714 and the newest 1942 – the year before the Army took possession.

Worbarrow Bay: The Swyre stream, which flows through Tyneham, joins the sea at the bay. Among those who lived by the shore was the village postman who doubled as a fisherman. The cliff to the north, known as Rings Hill, rises to 650 ft.

Lulworth Castle was built in 1608 and has been in the hands of the Catholic Weld family since 1641. From the top of the castle there is a view of the sea through an opening in the hills. The building was gutted by fire in 1929 and restoration is only now nearing completion by English Heritage. Below the castle is the medieval tower of St Andrew's church. Hidden behind the castle is the private Catholic chapel built in 1786 to look like a garden temple. This, the oldest post-Reformation Catholic church, was allowed by George III only on condition that it was disguised. At this time Edward Weld's widow Maria (also known as Mrs Fitzherbert) had secretly married the Prince Regent in a cere-mony later declared invalid. Soon after the chapel had been inspected by the King it was the setting for the secret consecra-tion of the first bishop for the newly independent USA (see page 31). In 1816 widower Thomas Weld let the castle to Sir Robert Peel and the Duke of Gloucester and went away to be ordained. As a cardinal he was noted for being the only one able to ride around Rome with his children. In 1830 the exiled Charles X of France spent two months at the castle.

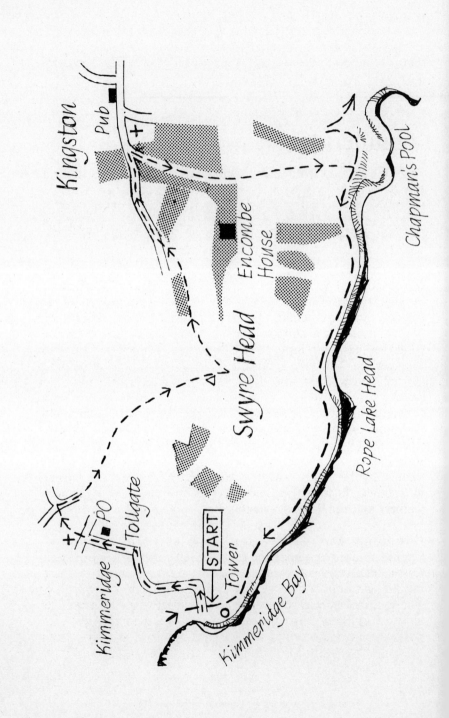

Kimmeridge, Smedmore Hill, Swyre Head, Kingston and Rope Lake Head

(Coast Path – Kimmeridge Bay to Chapman's Pool)

Introduction: The hill above Kimmeridge offers a spectacular view down onto the remote village as well as across to Corfe Castle and Bournemouth. Behind Swyre Head, Purbeck's highest point, is a stately home hidden in a valley. Over the centuries many attempts have been made to bring industry to Kimmeridge but only agriculture has succeeded, so preserving the area for walkers who enjoy vistas denied to motorists.

Distance: A 9 mile circular route with one steep climb. Map: OS Outdoor Leisure 15 (Purbeck).

Refreshments: Kimmeridge post office serves teas daily including weekends. The Scott Arms at Kingston, which has a superb view down on to Corfe Castle, serves food fast and welcomes walkers and families at lunchtime.

How to get there: Kimmeridge lies in a valley just south of Steeple and is reached by road from Wareham and Corfe Castle. Parking in the village is extremely limited and visitors should continue south on the toll road to Kimmeridge Bay where there is plenty of parking space. Public transport is almost non-existent (one bus one way on Thursdays) but walkers can take Wilts & Dorset bus 143 or 144 from Wareham BR station to the Scott Arms at Kingston and start the walk at the halfway point. (Telephone 0202 673555 for details of timetable.)

Coast Path: Follow this walk as far as Houns-tout cliff but walkers wishing to stay on the coast should go up the steps to the Clavell Tower and follow the cliff top path to Houns-tout cliff where there is a seat facing west.

The path descends Houns-tout by steps and, to avoid dangerous cliffs, turns inland on a new path to join a metalled road. On reaching buildings, the way is south uphill to follow a stone wall (left) which has a stile just before a memorial picnic area (see Walk Seven).

The Walk: The walk starts at Kimmeridge Bay. Follow the metalled toll road into the village and continue up the main street. At the north end by Kimmeridge Farmhouse (left) leave the road and continue ahead up the steps and on to a path running through the churchyard. After a kissing gate climb the steep hill to a gap in the trees near the top. Here look back for the first panoramic view of the walk before continuing to a stile by a road junction.

Walk up the road opposite and after a short distance go right onto a track. Beyond a gateway the track runs alongside open ground as it climbs Smedmore Hill. There is a first view of Corfe Castle over to the left. Look back to see Steeple church. Down to the right is a view across Kimmeridge. The track follows a stone wall and after three more gateways becomes enclosed. Here there is a view on the seaward side down onto Smedmore House.

Where the track swings left continue ahead through a small wooden gate. Beyond the next narrow gate there is the Swyre Head Ordnance Survey trig point.

Only to enjoy the view, continue ahead past the trig point and over the stile to a burial mound where there is also a seat.

The walk continues to the left before the trig point to follow a stone wall (left). Soon Polar Wood is behind the wall with Encombe House visible down in the valley to the right. Ahead is Kingston church tower and an obelisk. Where the wood falls away go through a gate and follow the path which at first heads towards the distant church tower before bearing leftwards down to a gate.

Go ahead between grand gateposts to a junction and turn right. The road runs across open country with a final view down onto Corfe Castle before passing through a wood on the edge of Kingston.

Just before reaching Kingston church and the village centre, the walk turns sharply right by the entrance to Kingston House. The path is waymarked 'Hounstout' and 'Encombe House'. Ignore the 'Private No Entry' sign intended for cars and follow the wide track through the wood.

Take the second turning on the right which soon passes a residence (left) where there are often eggs and fruit for sale. At the end of the lane go over the first of a series of stiles and follow the stone wall (left). There is a view (right) over to the obelisk and down onto Encombe House and its lake. At the fourth stile, where there is a view (left) over to Worth Matravers and St Aldhelm's Head, there is a stone seat facing west. The Clavell Tower at Kimmeridge can be seen 2½ miles away at the end of the walk.

At the seat go right down the very steep path which runs down into the wooded valley where a stream joins the sea at a waterfall. The coast path immediately begins a long climb and soon runs close to a fence (right). At the top there is a view up to Swyre Head. The path runs more gently downhill, crossing two gullies, before passing a stile (leading to a Swyre Head path) and reaching Rope Lake Head which is so slight that it is easily passed by.

Ahead there is a view of the tower which will be lost for a while as the path descends. Further ahead can be seen the white cliffs beyond Kimmeridge. There are more footbridges over gullies each side of Clavell's Hard before the path winds gently uphill again. Jutting dangerously over the cliff is a set of track points from the 19th century shale tramway. There is another gully with a steep climb before the path gently bears round to the Clavell Tower on Hen Cliff above Kimmeridge Bay.

Pass inland of the tower and at once go right down a path which becomes stepped to reach the start of the toll road up to the village.

Historical Notes

Kimmeridge Bay, being part of the Smedmore Estate, has a toll road from the village. The Clavell family bought the estate in 1554 and the present owner, Colonel Mansell, is a descendant. Smedmore House, the family seat a mile to the north east, dates from the early 17th century when Sir William Clavell was trying to exploit the shale found in the cliffs. His attempts to extract alum failed and his cob harbour was finally destroyed during a storm in 1745. The shale was once known as Kimmeridge Coal but its 'bad eggs' smell when burned made it unpopular. Very occasionally it is subject to spontaneous combustion – in 1973 part of the cliff at Clavell's Hard was found smouldering. During numerous attempts in the 19th century to make use of shale, a mine was opened on the eastern cliff and tramways were laid. A short distance to the west of the lonely mineworkers' cottages is the site of Britain's first successful oil well, which was sunk in 1959.

Kimmeridge: The stone thatched cottages date only from the 17th and 18th centuries but the church has a Norman doorway and a partly 15th century bellcote. The stone in the porch is believed to be a cheese-press. This has always been a thinly populated area but since the estate was owned by Cerne Abbey from Saxon times until 1539 it is thought that the monastery supplied a priest. In the 18th century there was a service only every other Sunday but now the parish is part of a large group ministry based at Corfe Castle. Outside the west end of the church is a line of coastguard gravestones. The village is proud of its Auxiliary Coastguard team which during a second call in one night in 1992 rescued a yacht skipper from the sea and winched both rescuer and victim up the cliff just east of Clavell's Hard.

Steeple church: Above its Norman doorway is an early 17th century carving of the Washington arms quartered with those of the local Lawrence family, commemorating the marriage of Agnes Washington to Edmund Lawrence. Later the USA flag was inspired by this 'stars and stripes' shield of President George Washington whose half-brother had the Dorset name of Lawrence.

Corfe Castle: There was a fortification in this Purbeck ridge gap in AD 978 when King Edward the Martyr was murdered at the gateway. The Norman castle stands on a natural chalk mound and remained a Royal fortress until 1572 when Elizabeth I sold it to Christopher Hatton, Lord Chancellor. In 1635 it was sold to the Lord Chief Justice Sir John Bankes whose family remained owners until 1982. The castle is now in the care of the National Trust. During the Civil War the Royalist Lady Bankes held out against a three year siege until 1646 when the Roundheads reduced the castle to its present ruined state.

Swyre Head, 682 ft high at the tumulus, is the highest point in Purbeck. Chris Jesty, a descendant of Benjamin Jesty (see page 48), claims that from here it is possible to see Dartmoor to the west and France to the south.

Kingston: The old church of St James, now converted into a residence, was built in 1833 by the 1st Lord Eldon of Encombe (see below) who employed his son-in-law architect, G.S. Repton. The present church, which from the east looks like a French cathedral, was given by the 3rd Lord Eldon in memory of his wife and built between 1873 and 1880 to a design by G.E. Street. This was the last time local stone was used extensively for a major Purbeck building. Street may also have been responsible for the attractive village pump outside the former post office. The oldest building is the pub which dates from 1650 but is now called the Scott Arms, Lord Eldon's family name.

Encombe House dates from at least the 1730s when an existing house was rebuilt. The mansion, hidden in Encombe Vale which is also known as the 'Golden Bowl', was later home of the 1st Lord Eldon who as a law student eloped with a banker's daughter and went on to become Lord Chancellor from 1807 to 1827. When Encombe caught fire one night, his first action was to rush into the garden and bury the Great Seal, which in the morning was not found until most of the garden had been dug up. Encombe is Thomas Hardy's 'Enkworth Court', the home of Lord Mountclere in *The Hand of Ethelberta*. The 40 ft obelisk on the hill was erected in 1835 in honour of the ex-Lord Chancellor's lawyer brother, Lord Stowell, whose judgements formed the basis of maritime law. The family still live here.

Clavell Tower was built as a summer house in 1831 by the Rev John Clavell of Smedmore House but the three storey folly was later used by coastguards as a lookout.

Worth Matravers, St Aldhelm's Head and Chapman's Pool
(Coast Path – Chapman's Pool to Seacombe Bottom)

Introduction: Today there is no sign of the many pylons which dotted the landscape during the Second World War when crucial radar research was carried out here. It is therefore a village which has improved in the last half of this century with the addition of a discreet car park away from the centre. The pub remains unchanged although the shop closed in 1992. Although this walk out to the chapel on the St Aldhelm's Head is short it offers good views.

Distance: A 4 mile circular route with one very steep climb. Map: OS Outdoor Leisure 15 (Purbeck).

Refreshments: Worth Matravers has two teashops, The Worth Tea Shop opposite the pond and Lynchet Tea Rooms at the Worth Farm Craft Centre (both closed winter weekdays), and The Square and Compass pub which serves fresh crab sandwiches.

How to get there: Worth Matravers lies off the Swanage-Kingston road, the B3069. There is a car park immediately outside the village at the northern entrance on the Kingston road. (A Wilts & Dorset bus, 144, leaves from Wareham station. Telephone 0202 673555 for details.)

Coast Path: Follow this walk from the stile in the stone wall

45

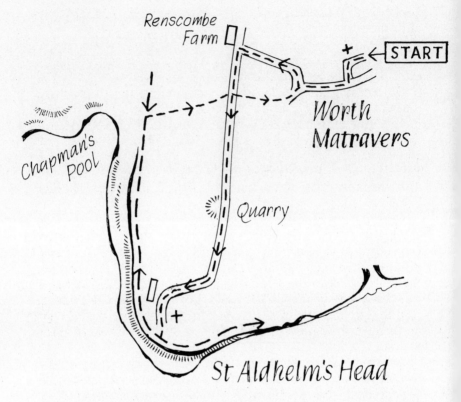

near the picnic area above Chapman's Pool to St Aldhelm's Head, but walkers wishing to stay on the coast should continue ahead to the chapel.

Continue on the path between the chapel and coastguard lookout. After a mile the path goes inland to descend into a valley known as Winspit. The way continues opposite and after a quarry returns to the cliff top but there is another detour to avoid a quarry at the next valley, Seacombe Bottom (see Walk Eight).

The Walk: From the pond walk past The Worth Tea Shop and the two stone figures of St Nicholas on the St Nicholas Court gateposts. Follow the road past the church and round a double

46

bend. (Do not go left downhill.) At Weston Farm keep right with the road to pass Old Harry Cottage.

At Renscombe Farm turn left onto a rough track which runs directly to St Aldhelm's Head a mile away. Before the Head the path passes the St Aldhelm's Head Quarry (right).

On reaching the Head pass between the coastguard cottages and the chapel to the Coastguard lookout. Turn right and stay close to the fence and away from the cliff edge. There are two seats facing the magnificent view along the coast. Beyond the stone seat, the path drops steeply into Pier Bottom to pass a stile (leading to a valley path running back to the outward path by the quarry). The walk continues ahead up the steep side of Emmetts Hill.

Once on top of Emmetts Hill, again keep near the fence as Chapman's Pool comes into view below. Immediately after crossing a stile above the Pool there is a new stone picnic table with matching seats protected by a fence. Continue past the table to follow the stone wall (on the right). After 300 yards go over a stile in the wall and follow the path ahead across a field to a second stile. Keep forward in the next field (but do not go through the gateway on the left) to cross the outward track at stiles.

Once across the track follow a partly enclosed path. (Be careful not to trip on the remains of the old fence posts.) At the far end cross a stile to go along a short path, lined by blackberry bushes, to another stile leading onto a farm track. Turn left to reach the road at Weston Farm and continue ahead into Worth Matravers.

Historical Notes

Worth Matravers is an unspoilt Purbeck village nestling in a fold to escape the worst of the sea winds. Worth means 'enclosure' and Matravers comes from John Matravers who held the manor for just 8 years from 1391.

The small Norman church was built about 1100 and has an impressive chancel arch. Over the entrance there is a rare early tympanum, illustrating the coronation of the Virgin, which sustained damage during a visit by Roundhead soldiers from Poole in 1646. Above the inside of the door is the mirror from the *Halsewell* which foundered at night just east of St Aldhelm's Head in 1786. It is said that the five girls among the drowned had looked in this glass to brush their hair before going to bed. The church is dedicated to St Nicholas, patron of sailors and children. His three ball symbol, used by pawnbrokers who also seek his protection, is on one of the kneelers. Another has the cow and needle of Benjamin Jesty who is buried to the north of the church. The tomb inscription states that he is 'noted for having been the first Person (known) that introduced Cow Pox by Inoculation'. This was in 1774 which is 24 years before the famous Edward Jenner published his findings. Mary Brown's tombstone on the east side states that her mother was 'personally inoculated for cow-pox by Benjamin Jesty'. In the churchyard's north east corner is a stone cross commemorating two victims of the *Treveal* disaster (see Chapman's Pool) – all the bodies found were briefly laid in a mass grave here, for just as the task was finished word came that the shipping company was paying for home burials. Nearby is a memorial to a young French naval lieutenant whose body was washed up in Chapman's Pool in 1917.

The garden below the village pond, and behind the rare green telephone box, once grew willows for the manufacture of lobster pots. Above the pond is the former village shop which closed in 1992 after 122 years. This was the centre of activity – post office, grocers, butchers, newsagent and tourist information office – run by a husband and wife team who held the secret of where to obtain the rare Dorset Blue Vinny cheese. Next door is Gulliver's Cottage, one of the many homes of smuggler Isaac Gulliver who liked to retain a local base to win over village confidence and support.

The Square and Compass is a former farmhouse which became The Sloop in 1752. The present name dates from about 1830. It has been run by the Newman family since 1907. Charles, grandfather of the present landlord, used to have long arguments here with artist Augustus John whose portrait by cartoonist Lowe is on the wall of the large room where the *Treveal* inquest sat. Opposite is Worth Farm which has become a craft centre and museum (open daily except winter weekdays).

Renscombe Farm is at the top of the path up from Chapman's Pool and its name is derived from a Saxon word meaning 'ravens valley'. Earlier this century the body of a girl was found embedded in the thick medieval walls of the farmhouse which once belonged to the Benedictine Cerne Abbey 25 miles to the north-west.

St Aldhelm's Quarry has been worked since the 12th century and has tunnels so close to the surface that brambles grow through the roof. The Haysom family has been quarrying here for 300 years. Recent work has included replacing the Studland village cross (see page 63) and relaying the floor of the Banqueting House in Whitehall. Purbeck marble is the top strata of limestone and Purbeck stone refers to the other layers. The Black Prince's tomb in Canterbury Cathedral is made of Purbeck marble. Purbeck stone was used in Winchester and Salisbury Cathedrals and in 1983 stone from here was used for Salisbury's new high altar. Following the Great Fire of London in 1666 there was a great demand for street paving and Purbeck flatteners remained popular until the building of the railways brought York flagstones south. The stone tiles on local cottages are flatteners rejected as being too thin for pavements.

St Aldhelm's Head rises over 400 ft above sea level and takes its name from Aldhelm, the first bishop of this part of Wessex, who died in AD 709 having built nearby Corfe church. The only buildings here are the Victorian coastguard cottages and the Norman chapel said to date from about 1140. The lonely St Aldhelm's Chapel was possibly built as a landmark for shipping by a father who watched his daughter drown as she sailed round the Head on her honeymoon. The cross on the chapel roof replaced what may have been a beacon holder in 1873. The 25 square ft building has its four corners pointing north, south, east and west – hence the altar across the eastern corner by the only window. The chapel was served by a chaplain appointed by the king but was abandoned at the Reformation to become a coastguard store and a cattle shelter. Late in the 18th century the buttresses were added on the southwestern side. In 1881 a coastguard's baby was baptised at the first service for over 300 years. Throughout the last century Worth villagers continued to process out to the chapel every Whit Thursday to decorate it and dance inside. This custom was probably a continuation of the annual observation of St Aldhelm's Day which falls around this time – 25 May. Since 1965 the chapel has been administered from Worth and now every Easter Day the dark building is lit by over a hundred candles for a well attended dawn Eucharist. Sunday evening services are held in summer.

Turning east from the coastguard lookout you can see the lighthouse at Peveril Point near Swanage. To the west there is Houns-tout with Swyre Head just beyond. Looking along the cliff, Clavell Tower indicates Kimmeridge Bay.

Chapman's Pool has been the scene of many sea rescues and tragedies. When the French barque *Georgina* was driven ashore in 1866 the master thought he was on the Isle of Wight. It is said that 2,400 bags of coffee and cocoa were brought safely on to dry land. The worst disaster here was the loss of the *Treveal* in 1920. The steamship was sailing from Calcutta to Dundee when she struck the hidden Kimmeridge Ledges during a January night and 36 crew members died trying to reach the beach. Fifteen bodies were never found and *The Daily Mirror* renamed the jute and seaweed strewn cove 'Dead Men's Pool'. The ship lies underwater in two halves a mile to the south west.

Swanage, Durlston Head, Dancing Ledge, Worth and Priest's Way

(Coast Path – Seacombe Bottom to Ballard Down)

Introduction: The coast path on the south side of Purbeck is the Isle's most remote cliff top walk. The circular route uses the coast for the outward trail and the older Priest's Way for the return. This is the best way round not only because there is a better view when walking east on the Way but also because this ancient path was used by the priest from Saxon times to walk from the mother church at Worth Matravers to Swanage where the church had only chapel status until as late as 1506. The cliffs are renowned for sea bird colonies which include Dorset's only puffins.

Distance: A 10 mile circular route. Map: OS Outdoor Leisure 15 (Purbeck).

Refreshments: Swanage has numerous pubs and teashops. Durlston Castle is open all year for coffee, lunches and teas. For Worth Matravers see Walk Seven.

How to get there: Swanage is at the end of the A351 south east of Wareham. Wilts & Dorset bus 150 from Bournemouth Square and 142, 143 or 144 from Wareham BR station. (Telephone 0202 673555 for details.)

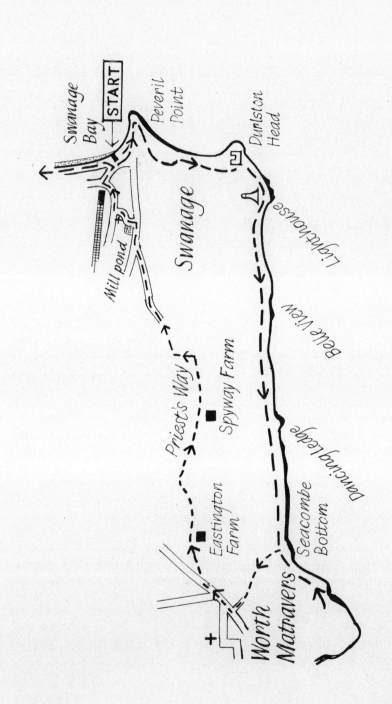

Coast Path: Follow this walk from Seacombe Bottom by turning left and walking up the valley. From the village ahead this walk is the ancient way to Swanage.

But walkers wishing to stay on the coast to reach Swanage should go right. Soon a fence (right) leads up the eastern cliff. After skirting two quarries there is Dancing Ledge. From here the path runs uphill and soon remains a little away from the cliff edge until reaching the Durlston Country Park.

Keep ahead to pass the lighthouse (left) and after a valley the path is enclosed to Durlston Castle. Pass the castle entrance (right) to follow a wide woodland path above Durlston Bay. The way narrows to climb steps to a road. Go right and at a bend right again to leave the road. Bear left to emerge on a grassy hill above Swanage. Go downhill and turn left for the town centre.

Walk to the far end of the promenade. The official coast path turns inland with the road and returns by way of Streche Road just beyond a modern church, but in good weather many walkers continue along the beach and rejoin the path at a little valley where there is a stream. Follow the cliff top path which rises up onto Ballard Down to a path junction near an Ordnance Survey trig point (see Walk Nine).

The Walk: Start at The Mowlem on Swanage seafront. Pass in front of the bookshop and over The Brook to go left to reach the sea. Follow the promenade past the terrace of traditional seaside houses and along the quay, where tram lines remain.

At the pier follow the road up the hill to go between bollards and join another road. After a double bend, near the Wellington Tower (left), the road reaches a gateway leading to Peveril Point.

Turn right to walk up the cliff path signposted 'Victorian Trail'. The way is soon across grass on the rapidly rising cliff. For safety keep behind the line of red warning notices to reach two stone seats at the top. Here there is a view across the bay to Old Harry with Bournemouth beyond.

At the side of the seats there is a path which bends inland to pass a stone gazebo (left) before reaching a gate at a road. Here

53

there are three London bollards. Turn left and after a short distance go down steps on the left between two blocks of flats.

A woodland path runs below several gardens and over a footbridge to start the gentle climb up to Durlston Head. Occasionally there is a glimpse of the sea. From a bend, where a seat offers a good view of the Isle of Wight, the path is known as the Isle of Wight Road. Ignore all turnings into the main part of Durlston Country Park and continue ahead to Durlston Castle.

Walk down the slope to the right of the castle. At a bend there is a path to the Great Globe but the walk continues to the right to follow a line of London bollards (left).

A very firm path walled off from the cliff edge runs ahead to pass the entrance to Tilly Whim Caves. Here on the left there is a view down onto the ledge. Where the wall ends keep carefully to the path for it runs very near the cliff edge as the way bends to the right at the top of a surprise valley. Go downhill and on climbing up the other side to below the lighthouse, look back to see into the Tilly Whim caves. At the top of the climb there is a view ahead to St Aldhelm's Head.

Soon the path is beside a wire fence (right). After ½ mile, where the way divides, take the left path down to a stile on the edge of Durlston Country Park. The path is now across the end of the National Trust-owned Belle Vue Farm where it hugs the inside of a wire fence (left). At the end go over a stile to cross an unfenced field to a further stile and pass a Naval nautical mile marker (left).

Beyond another stile the path is by the fence (left) but at a further stile it runs some distance above the fence. Later the way curves inland above Blackers Hole and through bushes. Later the way opens out to run away from the fence until reaching a stile. Now the path is near a fence (left) before running steeply downhill and uphill to a stile. Here there is a view down onto Dancing Ledge.

The path runs gently downhill by the fence. There may be a muddy stream to negotiate. At the bottom cross a stile ahead and continue forward. After a short distance look back for another view down onto Dancing Ledge. Continuing ahead there is a view of the strip lynchets (medieval field system) on the side of a hill.

Beyond a stile above Topmast Quarry, the path enters Eastington farmland. There is another stile above a second cliffside quarry – known as Hedbury – and a couple more stiles before the path turns inland with a fence (left) at Seacombe.

On joining a stony path continue up Seacombe Bottom. Pass the waymarked steps (left) taking the coast path westward. Soon the valley divides. Bear left up the left hand valley – a footbridge carries the path over a ditch. At the end of this long grassy walk there is a stile by a small gate. Climb up the steep hill to a second stile on the skyline – there are steps for the last few yards.

Once at the top continue ahead as a view of St Aldhelm's Head and Worth (right) opens out. Cross a stone stile and head for a point just above the second house across the valley. On the way bear slightly over to the right to find a faint path running down between strip lynchets and up to a stile. Follow a narrow passage and go right at a rough track to reach the centre of Worth Matravers. The pub is up the road to the right.

Walk eastwards out of the village to pass between The Square and Compass and the Craft Centre. Go beyond the houses and on reaching a barn go over a stile opposite (right). Bear half left to cross stiles at a concrete road. At a further stile head towards a gate on the far side of a field which offers a view (right) down to Seacombe Bottom.

At the wooden farm gate go over the stone stile at the side. This is where the footpath officially joins the old Priest's Way bridlepath which can be seen as a faint track coming from the north west. Continue ahead on the now well used track to pass Eastington Farm (right). There are several gateways on the Way and most have a stile at the side. On passing through a quarry there is the first view down onto Swanage.

The track passes some cottages (left) on the edge of Aston. Keep ahead where the way divides at a turning to Dancing Ledge. On meeting a stony crosstrack (linking Langton Matravers with Dancing Ledge) continue forward. Here the

Way passes into the grounds of Spyway Farm where it runs under a lonely tree. Before the Way becomes walled there may be an old iron gate to negotiate. Here there is a fine view of Ballard Down (left).

When the walled stretch ends at a gate continue ahead but where this much used stretch of track bears left keep forward through a gateway. The Way runs along the back of a farmhouse. Bear round to the front of the building and down its approach to cross a cattle grid and meet another lane.

Turn right and after a short distance go over the stone stile on the left by a gateway whilst the road swings to the right. Cross a field and go over another stone stile by a gate to walk along an enclosed stretch of the Way. At the end an old gate leads into a field. Keep ahead along its side to a stile by the entrance to Belle Vue Farm (left).

Go through the gate opposite and turn left to follow a grassy track downhill. There is another gate just before the way bears right to run alongside a row of houses. The path becomes enclosed by bushes before widening out between Swanage housing.

At a road turn left and follow the road, ignoring all turnings including Cow Lane, as it swings to the right and runs along the top of the valley. The road drops down to narrow and join another by a shop (left). Continue ahead and just after The Black Swan (right) go left at a memorial cross down to the millpond and Swanage church.

This is the end of Priest's Way. To reach the seafront follow the road round to the right and pass the east end of the church to the main road. Turn right with The Brook to a main road junction by the railway and bus station. Station Road to the right leads to The Mowlem.

Historical Notes

Swanage: In the 19th century huge amounts of stone were sent by sea to London by John Mowlem (founder of Mowlem construction) and his nephew George Burt. On return trips the ships' ballast was often old street furniture so today bollards with London inscriptions are found scattered around the town. The Wellington Tower near Peveril Point once stood near London Bridge station. Swanage Town Hall frontage is the 17th century Mercers' Hall from Cheapside.

An early holidaymaker was Queen Victoria who came as a 16 year old princess to spend a night at the Royal Victoria. Later she sent her 14 year old son, the future Edward VII, to stay during a secret walking tour but he was given only a sofa by the landlord who declared he had no time for boys. When he saw the cheque he vowed to be polite to all guests whatever their appearance.

George VI came here during the war using the railway which had opened in 1885. Although closed in 1972 by BR it has re-opened as the Swanage Railway and will eventually run again beyond its existing Corfe Castle terminus to the main line at Wareham.

Swanage was 'Knollsea' to Thomas Hardy who in *The Hand of Ethelberta* set the wedding of Ethelberta in the church here. Artist Paul Nash lived at 2, The Parade (1935–6) whilst writing and illustrating the Dorset Shell Guide. Among politicians who went to school here were Michael Foot and his famous brothers, as well as Shirley Williams and David Mellor.

The seaside town retains its charm largely thanks to the House of Lords' refusal in 1987 to approve a Bill for a yacht marina which had been rejected in a local referendum.

Durlston Castle was built of local stone in 1887 by George Burt who was 'King of Swanage' according to Hardy, who lunched here in 1892. Burt had hoped that the top floor would be a Lloyds' signal station but the offer was never taken up. The castle, intended as the restaurant and tearoom it remains, was also to have been the climax of a large development but fortunately the huge grounds have become a country park. The stone bollards at the castle entrance were trial runs for those placed in Trafalgar Square.

The Great Globe: The 40 ton Portland stone globe was created at Mowlem's Thames-side yard at Greenwich. There are 15 pieces which were assembled here in 1887.

Tilly Whim Caves: Having completed the castle in 1887 George Burt opened the former quarry to the public in the same year. They were closed in 1976 on safety grounds. A 'whim' is a crane which lowered stone into a boat. John Mowlem began his working life here as an apprentice.

Dancing Ledge, a stone platform left from quarrying, is washed by high tides which replenish a small man-made swimming pool. This famous Dorset beauty spot, reached only on a 2 mile round walk, passed into the hands of the National Trust in 1992.

Seacombe: The cliffside quarries on the west side of Seacombe Bottom were in use from 1700 until 1930 when the dramatic 12 ft high entrances were abandoned. These workings, the deepest on the coast, are now extremely dangerous. In early 1991 six wild ponies were brought from Exmoor by the National Trust to establish a herd for grazing Seacombe Bottom alongside the cattle and sheep. The mixed grazing should maintain shorter grass suitable for the early spider orchid and other wild flowers.

Worth Matravers: See Walk Seven.

Eastington Farm, owned by the National Trust, once belonged to Christchurch Priory.

Spyway Farm was bought by the National Trust in 1992 after being owned by the Curtis family for many years. Some of the drystone walls on the 190 acre farm were built by Napoleonic prisoners.

Studland, Ballard Down and Old Harry Rocks

(Coast Path – Ballard Down to Branksome Chine)

Introduction: The countryside around Studland is outstandingly beautiful with extensive views and colonies of gulls and cormorants along the cliffs. Even so, the area is being improved by the National Trust which inherited huge tracts of land here in 1982. New hedges and woodland are being planted and over 200 acres have been allowed to return to heathland and downland. The open land at Old Harry has reverted to natural grassland for the first time since it was ploughed close up to the coast path in 1954. At the same time restriction on pesticides and fertilizers is encouraging bird and wildlife.

Distance: A 4 mile circular route with one very steep climb. Map: OS Outdoor Leisure 15 (Purbeck).

Refreshments: Studland Tea Room is next to Studland Stores on the corner of the main road and School Lane. The Manor House Hotel is open for all meals including tea, and The Bankes Arms serves lunches. The beach café is open all the year and sells Purbeck ice cream, made on a nearby farm with double cream.

How to get there: Studland is on the B3351 Corfe Castle to Sandbanks Ferry road which is a toll road at its north end beyond the village. Bus 150 runs daily from Bournemouth Square and Branksome BR station to Swanage via Studland (0202 673555 for details).

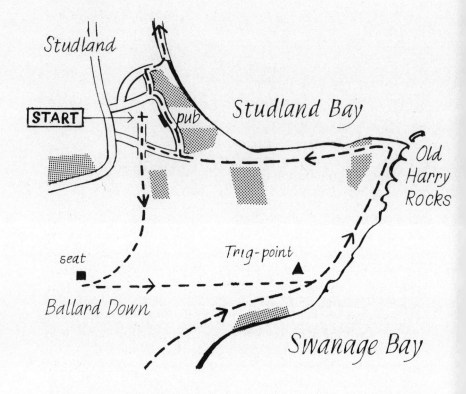

Coast Path: Follow this walk from the east end of Ballard Down – near the trig point. In Studland turn right to pass The Bankes Arms and go right at both junctions to reach the beach. Turn left to follow the beach, which passes through a nude bathing area, to the official end of the Dorset Coast Path at Sandbanks Ferry.

On the far 'mainland' side the route continues as the unway-marked Bournemouth Coast Path. Go ahead to the road junction and turn right. Later the road runs alongside Poole Harbour. Just beyond the Sandbanks Hotel go right through a public garden and right again to reach the seafront. Turn left and stay on the promenade as far as Branksome Chine (see Walk Ten).

60

The Walk: The walk begins at Studland church which can be reached by walking down School Lane at the side of the Studland Tea Room and Stores and turning up a footpath on the left beyond the vicarage. There is also a footpath to the church from the side of the National Trust car park by The Bankes Arms.

From the church door take the lane ahead to the junction by the village cross. Keep ahead along the side of Manor Farm Dairy House. The track is rough at first but soon has a metalled surface which greatly improves as the road rises to pass the Glebeland Estate houses. Look back from time to time at the improving view.

When the road has swung right to lose its tarmac surface do not continue to the cottage but at once bear half left to go through a gate. Follow a rising footpath up the side of Ballard Down. There is a dramatic view across Studland Bay and Poole Harbour (right). Later the path swings leftwards across the open downland to a wooden gate by a stone marked 'Rest and be Thankful'. Across a gate is a view down onto Swanage.

Go through the gate and turn left. (There may be a redundant stile.) Follow the wide short grass path along the top of Ballard Down. After nearly ½ mile there are two burial mounds to the right. Keep forward through the gate ahead to reach an Ordnance Survey trig point.

Go ahead for a few yards to meet the Dorset Coast Path at a junction and turn left. It is important not to stray from the main worn path which is back from the dangerous cliff edge. After 400 yards the path bears leftwards at another corner to run gently downhill towards Handfast Point, better known as Old Harry Rocks. On the way there is a view down onto two lonely chalk stacks known as The Pinnacle and Haystack.

At Old Harry the path turns west to follow Studland Bay. After passing through Studland Wood, the path is some distance from the cliff top for ¾ mile. At a junction do not bear left through the gate or go sharp right on the waymarked path down to the beach. Instead go ahead along an enclosed path which passes a lonely house in spacious cliff top grounds (right).

A wooden gate leads onto a lane which runs ahead down to a road where there are toilets and handy maps (right). The road ahead leads up to the village cross near the church but turn right past the toilets for The Bankes Arms.

Historical Notes

Studland: The tiny church is suitably dedicated to St Nicholas, patron of sailors and children. Traces of the 8th century Saxon church, probably built under St Aldhelm's direction (see page 49), can be seen in the north wall but the present building is predominantly Norman. Most impressive are the round Norman arches inside, which show signs of subsidence – the tower was never completed due to misgivings as work progressed. Extensive restoration was needed in 1881–3. The gallery had been added a century earlier when wood became available from a shipwreck.

In the churchyard is the tomb of Sergeant William Lawrence (near porch) who fought at the Battle of Waterloo and, as the back of the stone indicates, married a Frenchwoman. The Lawrences ran The Bankes Arms when it was called The Duke of Wellington after William's commander. The Bankes family of Kingston Lacey near Wimborne were the local landowners until the family died out in 1982 and the estate passed to the National Trust.

The Manor House Hotel was built about 1825 as a seaside villa for George Bankes. The Gothic style building, with medieval carvings in the dining room and a 16 acre garden, has been run as a hotel by the Rose family since 1950.

Children's author Enid Blyton owned nearby Studland golf course and spent many holidays on the Isle of Purbeck. Several 'Famous Five' stories are set here and 'Mr Plod' in the Noddy books was based on the village policeman. Other literary figures attracted to Studland include Virginia Woolf who first came in 1909 and hired a bathing costume. Later she stayed at 2, Harmony Cottages along from the Post Office. Lady Ottoline Morrell, also part of the Bloomsbury group, spent an illicit holiday with Bertrand Russell at Cliff

End Cottage down the private lane at the side of The Bankes Arms' garden.

A more recent private visitor was the Princess of Wales who walked along the beach and called in at the post office one winter day. It was over Studland Bay that Prince Charles made his first parachute jump in 1971.

In 1976 the village cross, which had only its Saxon base remaining, was restored. The design and carving were carried out by Trevor Haysom (see page 49). On the east side Christ stands above a geometric double helix representing DNA, a bomb and Concorde.

Rest And Be Thankful stone: The Purbeck stone seat was placed on top of Ballard Down in 1852 by Bow Street magistrate and legal writer Davide Jardin who lived in Swanage. His initials can be found carved on the end.

Ballard Down: From the top you can look across to Poole and Bournemouth to the north as well as down onto Swanage to the south. Sometimes the whistle of a steam engine can be heard from the Swanage-Corfe railway and smoke can be seen tracing out the line. Beyond Swanage Bay is the outline of Durlston Castle. To the east is the Isle of Wight which looms large on a clear day. The island's high ground is the continuation of the Ballard Down chalk ridge which was once joined. In summer this spine path is a good place to see butterflies – red admirals and painted ladies.

Old Harry Rocks, or Handfast Point, is a magnificent viewpoint which not surprisingly was defended in Tudor times although a last trace of the fort fell into the sea in 1770. The Spanish Armada's *San Salvadore* lies nearby in Studland Bay having sunk whilst being taken by the English from Weymouth to Portsmouth. The main detached 'rock' is called 'No Man's Land' and the gap is known as St Lucas Leap after a greyhound which attempted to jump the space when chasing a hare. 'Old Harry' stands furthest away without his 'wife' who was lost during a storm in 1896. The ashes of writer H.G. Wells were scattered from a boat off this point in 1946.

Studland Wood: The hazel was probably planted to produce timber for fencing and fuel for bread ovens. In 1991 coppicing was revived here after a lapse of over 50 years but only small sections are being tackled each year so as not to change the feel of the wood too quickly. The coppiced hazel provides spars for thatching.

Bournemouth, Branksome Chine, Branksome and Bournemouth Chine

(Coast Path – Branksome Chine to Southbourne)

Introduction: The sandy Bournemouth cliffs afford a view of Poole Bay from Hengistbury Head in the east to Sandbanks in the west with the Isle of Purbeck opposite. Here in Bournemouth the walker is on the Bournemouth Coast Path, which continues the Dorset Coast Path from the Poole Harbour entrance at Sandbanks to just beyond the modern county boundary. The patches of heather and bracken are remnants of the Dorset heathland which once reached to the cliff top. One of the dwindling number of sand lizards may occasionally be seen. The most well known feature is the pine woodland which runs along the cliff and up the chines – local name for valleys. This walk takes the coast path across the deep chine entrances and explores two major ones.

Distance: An easy 6 mile circular route with opportunities to break off at bus stops or the BR station at Branksome, which could be an alternative starting point for those coming from outside the area. Maps: Estate Publications Bournemouth Street Plan, OS Pathfinder 1301 (Wimborne and West Bournemouth).

Refreshments: The Argyll Clifftop Café between Middle and Alum Chines is open daily in summer. The Branksome Chine Solarium Café on the promenade is open daily in summer. In

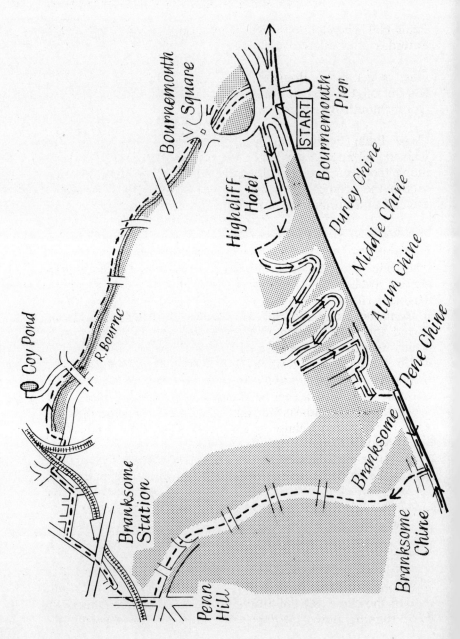

Bournemouth Square

Highcliff Hotel

START

Bournemouth Pier

Durley Chine

Middle Chine

Alum Chine

Dene Chine

Branksome

Branksome Chine

Coy Pond

R. Bourne

Branksome Station

Penn Hill

Penn Hill The Spinning Wheel teashop is open daily except Saturday afternoons and Sundays.

How to get there: Bournemouth is at the end of the A338, turning off the A31 at Ringwood. Yellow Buses run between Bournemouth BR station and the pier.

Coast Path: Follow this walk from Branksome Chine but walkers wishing to stay on the coast should continue ahead along the promenade to Bournemouth Pier. Beyond Bournemouth the promenade is continuous to near Point House at the end of Southbourne (see Walk Eleven).

The Walk: Start at Bournemouth Pier. After looking out to sea turn right to walk up the long slope leading to the West Cliff. The wide path passes the side of the BIC and the Bay Hotel before reaching the cliff lift almost opposite the landmark Highcliff Hotel.

Continue along the cliff top where there are wide lawns. Avoid the path leading to steps and follow the main path which bends round the edge of Durley Chine.

Go down steps but when they divide take the right fork. Cross the chine road and climb the steps opposite a road. Turn left and after a short distance there is Cherry Tree Walk which in blossom time is a delightful short cut on this walk. The road bends round Falaise to the cliff but soon turns inland to avoid Middle Chine.

Continue past the west end of Cherry Tree Walk to cross the chine on a bridge bearing the Bournemouth borough arms. At once go left along West Overcliff Drive which runs along the side of Middle Chine. The road bends round Argyll Gardens for another sea view before turning north alongside Alum Chine. After ¼ mile turn left to cross the chine on a high suspension bridge.

On the far side the bridge meets a road at a sharp bend. Go left along Studland Road past a line of hotels perched on the side of the chine. At the Studland Dene Hotel cross the steep road running down into the chine and go up steps almost opposite to find the cliff and a fine view of the bay.

Turn right up the cliff to reach some of the few cliff top private gardens in Bournemouth. Go round the first house into Sandbourne Road and turn right down a narrow passage next to number 17. The path turns left and descends down steps into Branksome Dene Chine.

Walk through the chine to the sea and turn right along the promenade passing below the Branksome Towers beach huts. On reaching Branksome Chine turn inland and cross the road to enter Branksome Chine Gardens.

Over the next 1¼ miles the valley stream is the guide to finding the way up the chine. The water is first on the left and then the right. Where the path widens and climbs, bear right and go over a crosspath to find the stream again over to the right. At a second bridge keep the water to the right and stay on this main track to pass the back of All Saints' church and reach Tower Road West. Cross over and continue on the path opposite which later runs alongside the stream. After Western Road a narrow path is beside the stream but later joins a wider path at the stream's double bend. Beyond Wilderness Road the way is past tennis courts and through a lonely archway. Cross two more roads – St Aldhelm's Close and Lindsay Road – keeping the stream on the right to reach Penn Hill.

Turn right along Archway Road to go under the Bourne-mouth–Poole railway line. Before reaching the modern St Joseph's church, go right up steps at the side of number 17. Follow the road and keep forward at a junction to reach the main Poole Road. Cross the road (using the crossing outside The Railway Hotel) to go ahead down Cromer Road. This road rises to cross an old level crossing.

Turn right into Gorleston Road and at the far end continue downhill with Bourne Valley Road to a roundabout. Go right to pass under the Gas Works Junction bridges. At a post box turn left down a narrow path leading into the Upper Pleasure Gardens.

The guide back to Bournemouth Pier is the Bourne stream running through a garden valley. It may be best to cross the bridge and keep the Bourne on the right for the final 2 miles.

Soon a road runs alongside skirting Coy Pond. Continue under the willows and cross Branksome Wood Road to find the largest uninterrupted stretch of river. After Prince of Wales Road there is a castellated tower above a point where the water is aerated as it passes through a narrow channel.

Beyond Queen's Road the gardens suddenly take on an urban feel with mown grass. After passing under the Wessex Way flyover, the Bourne is over to the right to avoid tennis courts. Shortly after the war memorial the stream flows through Paradise Garden where there is a rare island. Cross the Square to follow the stream through the Lower Pleasure Gardens to the seafront where the Bourne can be seen entering the sea from a pipe to the east of the pier.

Historical Notes

Bournemouth dates from 1810 when The Royal Exeter Hotel was built as a seaside residence on the side of the chine by Lewis Tegonwell who is shown on the hotel sign. St Peter's church was designed by G.E. Street and has a chapel commemorating hymn writer John Keble who died at Brookside (next to the White Heritage Hotel) opposite the pier. In the churchyard is the heart of the poet Shelley, buried in the Wollstonecraft tomb (top of the steps), which was removed from London under the supervision of the young Thomas Hardy. The author later featured the town as Sandbourne in his novels including *Tess of the d'Urbervilles*.

Highcliff Hotel was a terrace of four houses turned into the Highcliffe Hotel in 1874 but the 'e' was later dropped to avoid confusion with Highcliffe village (see page 84). Guests have included R.L. Stevenson, Beatrice Webb, Madame Prokofiev, U Thant, Rudolf Schwarz, Nureyev and Prime Ministers Wilson, Callaghan, Thatcher and Major. In 1940 Clement Attlee presided over a meeting in the basement which led to the formation of the Churchill coalition government. The Highcliff became 'The Majestic' for the television version of Agatha Christie's *The Body In The Library*.

Falaise, built in 1913, was the home of pioneer aviator Sir Alan Cobham.

Alum Chine takes its name from a short-lived Tudor alum works. Robert Louis Stevenson lived in a house at the top of the chine where he finished *Kidnapped* and wrote *The Strange Case of Dr Jekyll and Mr Hyde* following a dream. The site is open daily (enter from Alum Chine Road). The suspension bridge was slung across the ravine in 1905 and features in Cyril Connolly's *The Unquiet Grave* where he wrote: 'Walking over the quivering planks I felt rooted, as in a nightmare, to the centre'.

Sandbourne Road recalls Hardy's name for Bournemouth, which meets the borough of Poole near the south end. Philip Hepworth was responsible for Cape Dutch style number 37 with its blue pantiles, completed in 1932. He may also have designed Viewpoint House, finished a year earlier at the far end of the road and home since 1970 of Max Bygraves.

Branksome Dene Chine was the scene of 18 year old Winston Churchill's accident in 1893. He was staying with his aunt Lady Wimborne in Alumhurst Road's Zetland Court which at the bottom of the garden had a rustic bridge across a corner of the chine. In a playful chase Churchill decided to jump off the bridge and slide down a tree. He fell 29 ft and was unconscious for three days. It was during his convalescence that Churchill met leading politicians and spent time in the Commons' gallery where he resolved to enter Parliament. In 1946 Neville Heath, who is depicted in Madame Tussaud's Chamber of Horrors, murdered Doreen Marshall here. Her body remained undetected under a rhododendron bush for a few days because Bournemouth police only searched up to the borough boundary which runs through the chine.

Branksome Chine was the start of a 5 mile smugglers' path to Kinson. In 1852 Sir Charles Packe built a mansion on the cliff top between Branksome and Branksome Dene Chine with a lodge in Westbourne. The gateway's pedestrian archway is now on the chine path near the tennis courts. The main house was the Branksome Towers Hotel from 1898 until 1973 when it was demolished. Guests who enjoyed the ambience of the wooded chine included Lloyd George who came as premier in 1921, Al Jolson, Gertrude Lawrence, the King of Afghanistan, the Duke of Windsor, the Beatles and Lawrence Olivier. Edgar Wallace set part of his novel *Mr Justice Maxell* at the hotel. More recently J.R. Tolkien, author of *The Hobbit*, lived at Woodridings in Lakeside Road. Pines do not predominate as in Bournemouth's chines although John Betjeman wrote: 'I walk the asphalt paths of Branksome Chine/In resin scented air like strong Greek wine'. A plaque at the chine entrance records the opening of the woodland walk in 1930 by Margaret Bondfield, the first female cabinet minister. The Solarium by the promenade was built in 1932 to reflect a continental bathing station.

Penn Hill is a 1920s village centre for the houses on the edge of Branksome. The butcher's retains its original frontage and the next door Bankes Bistro is easily recognisable as the old fishmonger's from its Carter tile fish decoration.

Cromer Road level crossing: Until 1948 a branch line left the main track just east of Branksome station to serve a pottery which was on the Homebase site from 1853 until 1981. The gateways remain by the road. In latter years the works was known as Redland Pipes and produced chimney pots, tiles and drains. The new approach road to Homebase and neighbouring giant stores has been named Redlands.

Gas Works Junction viaducts were built in the 1880s across the Bourne Valley to carry the Bournemouth-Poole railway line and the curving loop into Bournemouth West station which closed in 1965. It is said that in one of the pillars of the disused viaduct is the body of a working pony which backed its cart too far and fell into the unfilled support.

Coy Pond, home of swans and ducks, was created in 1886 when the Bourne Bottom branch of the Bourne was piped under the new railway embankment to the north. Despite its name the pond was never a decoy pond for entrapping wildfowl.

Southbourne, Double Dykes, Hengistbury Head and Wick

(Coast Path – Southbourne to Highcliffe Castle)

Introduction: This tip of Poole Bay, better known by its unofficial name of Bournemouth Bay, was inhabited long before Bournemouth and Poole. Now, as the bay's only real rural coastline, it is being carefully conserved. From the headland viewpoint it is possible to survey Purbeck and Christchurch Bay. One short stretch of this easy circuit touches the urban sprawl but it does so only at the spot associated with one of Britain's most famous names.

Distance: A 5 mile circular walk with one steep climb. The walk could easily be completed in half a day but there are so many opportunities to pause at viewpoints that it could be a day's outing. Maps: OS Outdoor Leisure Map 22 (New Forest) and Estate Publications Bournemouth Street Plan.

Refreshments: Point House at the start of the walk is open daily in summer. The Double Dykes Café, by the Ranger's Information Office, is open in summer and holiday periods.

How to get there: Hengistbury Head is on the edge of Southbourne at the eastern end of Bournemouth off the A35. Point House is near the car park on the Southbourne coast road. Yellow Buses 12 (Summer Coastal Service), 22 from Pokesdown BR station, 25.

Coast Path: Follow this walk as far as the bottom of the steps behind Hengistbury Head. Instead of passing Holloway's Dock

73

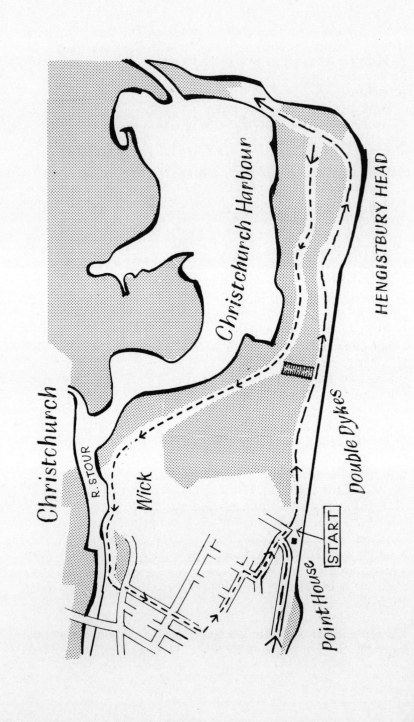

Christchurch

R. STOUR

Wick

Christchurch Harbour

HENGISTBURY HEAD

Double Dykes

Point House

START

go right on the access road to the Mudeford sand spit. A ferry (in summer) runs across the Christchurch Harbour entrance to Mudeford.

Walk along the quay and follow the path in front of Sandhills caravan park. At a road the way continues along the top of a low cliff and later joins a narrow promenade. At Steamer Point keep along the beach. (In bad weather or at very high tide walkers may wish to take the inland footpath which crosses a golf course and joins a main road near Highcliffe Castle.) There is an established path below the cliffs from the Highcliffe Castle beach entrance (see Walk Twelve).

The Walk: Point House is the last building on the Bournemouth bay cliff top before Hengistbury Head. To reach this viewpoint leave Point House café and whilst the road swings away inland take an indistinct path running parallel to the low cliff. The sea view is briefly obscured as the way runs behind sand dunes. Two posts mark the continuing path which is later close to the now diminishing cliff.

A newly restored section of cliff takes the coast path round the end of Double Dykes and across grassland to the steps leading up to the Ordnance Survey trig point on Hengistbury Head.

Follow the path past the coastguard station and continue round the headland. Ignore all turnings. On the way there is a view down onto Quarry Pond and ahead are The Needles on the tip of the Isle of Wight. The path swings north to steps above the Mudeford sand spit. Descend and bear left to join a road.

Here there is little traffic apart from the regular land trains linking the road at Double Dykes with the beach huts. Almost at once the road passes Holloway's Dock before running through woodland. At a double bend there is a view ahead of Christchurch Priory. When the road is alongside Christchurch Harbour it is possible to look northeast towards the harbour entrance.

Ahead along the road is a thatched barn. On approaching the bus route terminus by the Ranger's office bear right. A signpost indicates 'Riverside walk to Wick Village'. On the way go

75

through one of the gaps onto the parallel road. At the end go through a kissing gate by the Outdoor Education Centre.

A path goes half left to pass a field corner and then run near a wooden fence (left). Later the path veers to the right hand corner of the field where there is a kissing gate. Keep across a second field to a bridge guarded by kissing gates. There is now a stony causeway over a field where Highland cattle may be grazing.

Soon after an iron kissing gate the path divides. Take the right hand fork and after a short distance turn right on a clear path which bears left to a kissing gate where hops can be found growing with blackberries. An enclosed path runs round to a second kissing gate on the edge of Wick. Pass in front of the entrance to the steep roofed River House to reach the river Stour.

Turn upstream and soon the path is briefly enclosed before crossing a natural draw dock and reaching Wick Ferry. Continue along the river bank which later has a gravelled path. When Tuckton Bridge comes into view take a left fork which leads up to a road.

Go left for a short distance and turn up Broadlands Avenue. Cross Broadway and walk up Southlands Avenue almost opposite. At the far end go left along a narrow straight path running between the playing fields of St Peter's School. The circular stone commemorating Charles Rolls can be seen in the far north west corner of the left hand field.

At the end of the path continue along Hengistbury Road and turn right up Wildown Road to Dalmeny Road. Opposite is a former boat house in front of Southbourne's coastguard cottages. Turn left to follow the road down to Point House.

Historical Notes

Double Dykes: The double bank is an Iron Age defence for a town otherwise surrounded by water. This was the most substantial of a series of settlements on the site from around 10,000 BC. At the time Double Dykes was thrown up there was even a mint here. Trading took place with Cherbourg for about 50 years. Later the Romans added to the port which was on the north side to take advantage of the more sheltered Christchurch Harbour. The area is now known as Barn Field and has just one building – the 18th century thatched barn which has double doors on two sides, so that when a horse-drawn cart pulled in the draught would separate the grain from the chaff.

Hengistbury Head was granted to Christchurch Priory in the 12th century. Later it passed to the Meyrick Estate (see page 83). In 1919 the Head was bought by Gordon Selfridge of Selfridge's fame who wanted to build a castle here. Philip Tilden completed the design for a huge 250 bedroom building but the 1929 stock market crash halted the scheme and the following year Bournemouth Corporation purchased the land.

The Ordnance Survey trig point is on the 100 ft high Warren Hill at the western end of the Head. Looking west there is the brick water tower in nearby Southbourne whilst the tower block flats can be seen 5 miles away on Bournemouth's East Cliff. To the east is Christchurch Bay with Hurst Castle at the far end out on a spit. To the south west is the Isle of Purbeck whilst the Isle of Wight lies to the south east. Immediately north is Christchurch Harbour with the Priory to the north west at the confluence of the rivers Avon and Stour. Behind is St Catherine's Hill where the priory was to have been built before a miracle moved the stone overnight to the harbourside.

Holloway's Dock was built in 1854 by Christchurch coal merchant John Holloway, who was shipping ironstone to Wales for smelting. Barges towed by steamers came from Southampton with coal for ballast. Until 1880 enormous amounts of ironstone were removed from the south east of the Head allowing sand to drift round onto the Highcliffe Beach and cause navigation problems. The open ironstone mine above the dock was dammed in 1976 to create Quarry Pond.

Wick Fields: Along the shoreline of Christchurch Harbour are reed beds where sedge warblers nest in summer before returning to West Africa. This area is an important landing point for migrant birds passing between the continent and the Avon Valley. In the fields long-haired Galloway cattle were introduced as recently as 1992 to help keep back encroaching scrub which would otherwise overwhelm the meadow flowers.

Wick is a hamlet and there is no church or pub, although the cottage on the green called Tranquillity was the shop. However, there was plenty of drink as this was a centre of smuggling in the 18th and even early 19th century. When consignments were due to arrive, the miller at Christchurch across the water would work late so that his light could guide boats across the harbour and up the Stour.

The miller's family also ran the ferry throughout the last century. The ½d fare saved a long journey upstream to the first crossing at Iford Bridge – the toll bridge at Tuckton was not built until 1882. The ferry, suspended in 1990 due to the need for a new landing on the Wick bank, is due to be restored shortly.

Opposite the ferry and dating from 1691 is Wick House where Lord Nelson is said to have dined. After the Battle of Trafalgar his bo'sun lived at the 17th century Riverside Cottage across the road. The tiny thatched cob and brick house was occupied by his granddaughter until 1982.

St Peter's School: In the north-west corner of the lower playing field is a memorial to Charles Rolls of Rolls-Royce fame who died here in a plane crash during an air show. The actual site is now Springfield Avenue but this grass is the last of the great open space on which the show was held in 1910. Rolls, aged 32, was flying a Wright biplane when it lost its tail, making him the first Englishman to die in powered flight.

Southbourne: Dalmeny Road is an old path to the sea from the coastguard cottages built in 1873. The Cellars Farm Road turning marks the site of the only other house here apart from the mid 18th century Stourcliffe in Ken Road. The area became Southbourne in 1870 when Dr Thomas Compton developed it as a health resort. For a short period there was a pier and promenade. Cliff top houses on the Southbourne Coast Road once had a road running on the south side – hence the back doors facing the road today.

St Katharine's church owes its dedication to Dr Compton who was inspired by the proximity of St Catherine's Hill and the Isle of Wight's St Catherine's Point seen on a clear day. Simon Preston, organist at the Duke of York's wedding, had his first organ lesson in this church.

In the 1890s the poet James Elroy Flecker spent his childhood holidays at Greenways at the north end of Warren Edge Road. He recalled Bournemouth's pines in his poem *Brumana*. The Southbourne Shell Garden at the beginning of the Overcliff Drive was begun in 1948 by ex-miner George Howard, who was looking for a way to protect his garden from all the sand blowing up from the beach and cliffs.

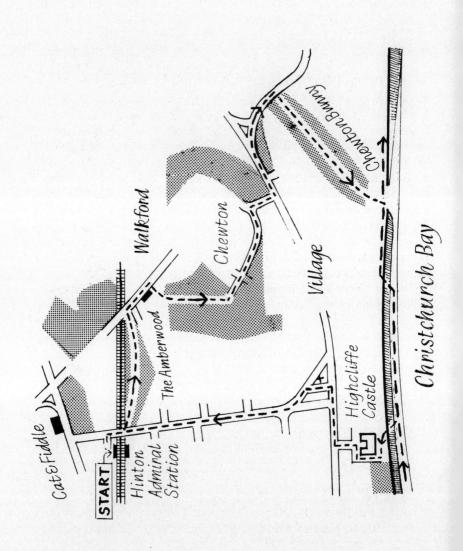

Hinton Admiral, Walkford, Chewton and Highcliffe Castle

(Coast Walk – Highcliffe Castle to Becton Bunny)

Introduction: Before reaching an unusual castle this walk follows the county boundary as it runs round the last village in Dorset and across ancient commons. Most of Cranemoor Common is in Hampshire and its footpath is also the county boundary. Since 1974 the Walkford Brook has been the eastern boundary on the coast instead of Branksome Dene Chine. The high cliff at Highcliffe was described in the 1820s as having 'one of the most beautiful views in the kingdom' and later Augustus Hare wrote of the castle setting as being 'paradise'.

Distance: A 5 mile circular route. Maps: OS Outdoor Leisure 22 (New Forest), Estate Publications Bournemouth Street Plan.

Refreshments: The Old Vicarage Hotel north of Hinton Admiral station is open for all meals including coffee and tea. The Cat and Fiddle on the main Lyndhurst road serves bar snacks in the old inn as well as meals in the extension added by the Harvester chain. The Amberwood in Walkford welcomes families. Highcliffe Castle's tearoom is open on fine summer afternoons.

How to get there: Hinton Admiral station is just south of the Cat and Fiddle on the A35 between Christchurch and the New Forest. BR to Hinton Admiral station. Wilts & Dorset bus 121 or 122 (telephone 0202 673555 for details).

Coast Path: Follow this walk from Highcliffe Castle but walkers

81

wishing to stay on the coast should continue eastwards on the paths below the cliff to Chewton Bunny.

Walk up the Bunny for a short distance before bearing right up the side of the valley on a path which leads to a caravan park. Turn right to reach the cliff top which is rapidly receding. Follow, at a safe distance, the edge of the cliff to reach the grass cliff top at Barton-on-Sea. On the far side of the shops turn down Becton Lane. Just beyond Farm Cottage (right) go half right on a narrow path onto Barton Common. Follow the path over a golf course to reach Becton Bunny (see Walk Thirteen).

The Walk: Leave Hinton Admiral station by the 'down side' and walk up to the road. Directly opposite are steps leading down to an enclosed path.

When the path divides take the left fork which runs through a tunnel of trees on Cranemoor Common. Beyond a crosspath and a stream, the path gently climbs to meet Ringwood Road at Walkford.

Turn right along the Walkford main street to pass Amberwood Lodge and soon The Amberwood pub. Just beyond the United Reformed church go right into Pinewood Close. Keep ahead and where the road ends take a metalled path which bears leftwards into the trees and across Chewton Common.

On meeting Chewton Common Road go left to pass The Cottage and the attractive Little Thatch on the corner of Upper Gordon Road. Continue over the crossroads and soon there is another enclave of thatched cottages (left). Pass Bramble Lane and Elphinstone Road to bear right with Chewton Common Road to meet Lymington Road on the edge of Highcliffe. Turn left along this main road to a roundabout.

At the roundabout cross the road to go right. The main road runs downhill to cross Walkford Brook. But just before the bridge veer off to the right on a narrow metalled path which runs into the trees of Chewton Bunny.

The path soon loses its firm surface and later meets the end of Mill Lane. Go left and soon there is a view down onto Mill

House. The path is gravelled before narrowing again and passing the first steps down to the stream which disappears into a pipe before joining the sea. Ignore a second set of steps and stay on the path which leads to further steps. Go down the flight and bear right where steps lead up to give a view of the sea and the Isle of Wight. Go ahead along the edge of the Bunny to the cliff top where there is the former Crow's Nest Café.

Leave the Bunny by turning west (right) past The Crow's Nest with a view to Hengistbury Head and Bournemouth beyond. Stay on the top of the cliff until just before the path turns inland. Go down the nearby wooden steps and continue westwards just below the cliff top.

(Walkers who prefer to take the path near the beach should turn inland behind the last groyne to find Highcliffe Castle.)

After a junction bear right with the 'Undercliff Walk' sign-post. This upper way briefly joins a wider path running down from cliff top residences before bearing off to the right and behind trees. Steps then take the way down to another path before further steps lead up to a zig-zag below Highcliffe Castle.

Follow the path up into the castle grounds and ahead towards the ruins. Turn left through the garden and round the outside of the castle to reach the front gateway. Keep forward to the main road and go right to pass The Old Hoy and reach the Lord Bute Restaurant.

Cross the road and go through the lychgate to pass St Mark's church. At the far end of the avenue go left along a road to a junction. Turn right and stay on the straight Hinton Wood Road to reach Hinton Admiral station.

Historical Notes

Hinton Admiral: The station, which opened in 1888 and not 1886 as suggested by the date in the brickwork, takes its name from the nearby mansion which is the seat of the 7th baronet Sir George Tapps-Gervis-Meyrick. In the early 1880s his great grandfather, also known as simply Sir George Meyrick, reluctantly agreed to the railway being cut through his estate but introduced Sunday closing at The Cat and

83

Fiddle when the Irish labourers started getting drunk. The ban continued until 1961. The pub name is probably a corruption of 'Catherine the Faithful'. Harvester, which recently bought the inn, was forced to reinstate the famous old sign. Sir George Meyrick retains the right to stop one train a day in each direction at the station. Among the first passengers using this station was William Gladstone who stayed at Highcliffe Castle in 1889. The grounds of Hinton Admiral have pines which are also found in profusion on Meyrick land in Bournemouth. In 1992 the estate contributed an oak for the rebuilding of Shakespeare's Globe Theatre on London's Bankside.

Walkford belonged to William de Walcford in 1195. The Amberwood Inn was the coach house for Amberwood House which stands behind in Amberwood Gardens – the gardener lived at Amberwood Lodge on the main road. When first converted in 1940 the coach house was a gentlemen's club but in 1967 it became a public house run by the club's founding family who remained landlords until 1991. Early in this century it was possible to see Studland from the top window of Amberwood House. The United Reformed chapel is a former Congregational chapel built in the 1830s.

Chewton Cottages along the north side of Chewton Common Road are whitewashed cob with thatched roofs and date from the late 17th century.

Highcliffe was the name chosen in 1892 to replace the confusing 'Newtown'. This included an area known as Slop Pond – Highcliffe Men's Club is built over the pond.

Chewton Bridge was built in 1901 and is England's earliest reinforced concrete bridge. This replaced a ford with a footbridge above the waterfall on the south side.

Chewton Glen is the land to the north above Chewton Bridge. The house dates from at least 1732 and from 1837 to 1855 belonged to the brother of novelist Captain Frederick

Marryatt. He wrote much of *The Children of the New Forest* whilst staying here in the 1840s. The residence became a hotel in 1962 and following expansion has won many awards. Guests have included Prince Philip, Prince Michael of Kent and Sir Edward Heath.

Chewton Bunny: A seaside valley here is not a 'chine' as in Bournemouth and on the Isle of Wight but a 'bunny'. There has been a mill since at least 1250 when it was owned by Christchurch Priory. The present Mill House dates from 1740.

The Crow's Nest is a former café closed by fire. The cliff top position was once part of the garden of Greystones whose tall chimneys can be seen above the new buildings. The Arts and Crafts style house by architect E.S. Prior was built in 1913 for the sister of Highcliffe Castle's owner.

Highcliffe Castle: The first building on the site was designed by Robert Adam in the 1770s for ex-premier Lord Bute who thought that this had 'the fairest outlook in England'. He died in 1792 following an accident whilst trying to reach a rare flower on the cliff. His 30 bedroom mansion was demolished but a generation later in 1835 his grandson Lord Stuart de Rothesay completed the Gothic castle which incorporated parts of ancient Norman buildings including Jumièges Abbey and St Vigor's church in Rouen. The oriel window on the south side comes from the room at the Grande Maison des Andelys where the King of Navarre died in 1562.

Lord Stuart's daughter, Lady Waterford, inherited the castle in 1867 and entertained numerous members of the royal family over 25 years. The future Edward VII arrived on the royal yacht which on another occasion was sent over from the Isle of Wight to take Lady Waterford to see Queen Victoria at Osborne. In 1891 the castle passed to Major Edward Stuart Wortley who welcomed the Duke of Connaught and in 1901 his brother Edward VII, who posed here for the first photograph of a monarch in a motor car.

The most significant guest was the Kaiser, who stayed for

three weeks in 1907 following his state visit. His catering arrangements were in the hands of Rosa Lewis, 'the Duchess of Duke Street', who brought food down daily from London on the royal train to Hinton Admiral. The Kaiser told his host that the English were 'as mad as March Hares' in not acknowledging him as their best friend. The publication of these remarks caused a storm in Germany and led to a distancing from the Kaiser of his ministers when war came in 1914.

After the Stuart Wortley family left in 1949 the castle became a seminary for a time but two serious fires have resulted in the need for the long restoration now being undertaken by English Heritage. Its ruined state has been the backdrop to several TV films including the 'Ruth Rendell Mysteries'.

The Old Hoy (167, Lymington Road) dates from about 1780 although it has been almost completely rebuilt. It used to be thatched and until 1868 was The Hoy pub. Customers in December 1838 included shipwrecked Russian sailors.

Lord Bute Restaurant occupies the lodges, built in 1779 to Robert Adam's designs, for Lord Bute's High Cliff House.

St Mark's church was completed early in 1843 as a gift from Lord Stuart de Rothesay of Highcliffe Castle. Gladstone and the Kaiser are among the famous castle guests who attended services. Another was Dame Nellie Melba who in 1926 sang Gounod's 'Ave Maria' from the organ loft. The original tiny 1840's building survives wedged between the two recent extensions. Gordon Selfridge, the founder of Selfridge's who rented the castle for short periods, is buried by the fence on the avenue side. In keeping with his financial collapse his stone is less ornate than his family's other two tombs. Behind is the depleted avenue once known as Ninepenny Avenue since each tree cost 9d when planted in 1843.

Milford-on-Sea, Hordle, Becton Bunny and Hordle Cliff

(Coast Walk – Becton Bunny to Milford-on-Sea)

Introduction: Although the cliff top path between Becton Bunny and Milford falls just outside Dorset it does not qualify as part of Hampshire's Solent Way coastal route which starts at Milford. Instead this most easterly section of the Christchurch Bay cliff is the final section of the Bournemouth Coast Path. Like west Dorset's Chideock (Walk One) it has not only a dramatic cliff which must be walked with care but also an abandoned village with a ruined church. Here on the east Dorset border the Isle of Wight becomes a powerful presence.

Distance: A 7 mile circular route with no steep climbs. Map: OS Outdoor Leisure 22 (New Forest).

Refreshments: Milford-on-Sea has 2 pubs, The Smugglers and The Red Lion. Around the green there are Polly's Pantry tearooms, the Bon-Bon Restaurant and Master Pink's fish and chip shop. On the seafront there is the Needles Eye Café. At Hordle the shop and The Three Bells are ½ mile to the left at the crossroads beyond the church.

How to get there: Milford-on-Sea lies on the B3058 between New Milton and Everton near Lymington. Wilts & Dorset bus 123 or 124 from Lymington bus station near BR station (telephone 0202 673555 for details).

Coast Path: Follow this walk from Becton Bunny. On reaching

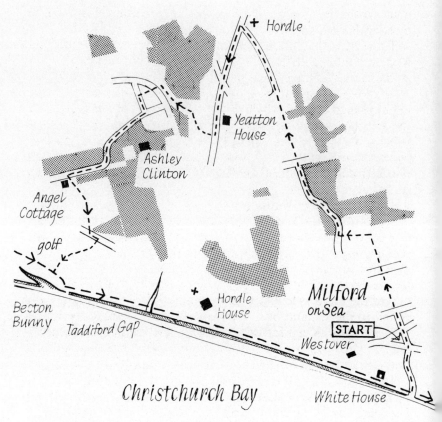

the Needles Eye Café at Milford-on-Sea the coast path continues as the waymarked Solent Way.

The Walk: Start on the north side of the green. Go up Church
Hill at the side of a thatched cottage. At the top turn into the
churchyard. Keep past the west end of the church on a path
which runs north out of the churchyard to become Cannons
Walk. Stay on this footpath as it crosses two residential roads.
At a kissing gate cross the road to continue up the concrete road
opposite. After an enormous glasshouse for tomatoes, the way
narrows. Here, running parallel in the trees, is the driveway to
Newlands Manor. The mansion remains hidden as the path

makes a sharp left turn. The way widens at Barnes Farm before meeting Barnes Lane.

Turn right to follow the lane downhill and past Barnes Manor House and its aviary (right). Just beyond the solitary Barnes Lane Cottage there is a road junction. To the right is a Newlands Manor gateway and lodge. Cross straight over the main road to a path, which is to be declared a byway. Go over the attached stile and follow the very narrow way which soon widens. Later there is another gateway as the lane further widens near a house. On meeting Sky End Lane (joining from the left) continue ahead for 1/3 mile to reach Hordle church (right) at the far end.

Turn left along Hordle Lane. Keep forward at a crossroads and soon there is Apple Court and Yeatton House on the left. Opposite is an unusual Gothic cottage. One field beyond this cottage turn right off the lane onto a footpath.

Follow the hedge (right) and at the end bear half right down the field keeping a lonely tree to the left. Just above the field corner there is a stile. Once in the wood follow the narrow path round to the left and over a wooden bridge spanning the infant Danes stream. Keep forward to a stile and climb a bank into a field. A path runs to the far left hand corner where a stile leads onto the main Highcliffe-Lymington road.

Turn right along the verge for a few yards before crossing the road (with care) to a stile up on the bank. A short path leads to a second stile at the end of a stopped-up road on Hooper's Hill. Turn left down the road passing a farm to a T junction where there is a milestone in the bushes (left).

Turn right along a road known as Angel Lane. Soon there is a view above the trees half right of the castellated water tower at New Milton. To the left is Ashley Clinton's Italianate tower. Later the lane passes a remote thatched cottage at the beginning of a treble bend. After the lane straightens out continue for 200 yards before turning left over a stile by a gate at the side of Angel Cottage. The path runs ahead to another gateway and ahead across a large field. The new Barton-on-Sea golf club can be seen in the distance to the right. On the far side cross a stile and bear half right across a field (there may be crops) to the corner at the end of a wood. Cross another stile and turn right down a gravel track to a road.

Turn left along the road's grass verge to pass a bus stop. Just before the road rises cross over to find a stile set back. This leads onto a golf course. Keep forward to follow a hedge line which has large gaps but remains the guide line across the course. Later there is a lonely stile just before running down to a path T junction near the sea. Turn left along a gravel track which bends round to the cliff top. To the right is Becton Bunny.

The walk continues to the left along a crumbling cliff top. There have been some dramatic falls and walkers should not stand near the cliff edge. After ½ mile the coast path runs down into Taddiford Gap.

On rising out of the valley there is an Ordnance Survey trig point in the field and behind can be seen the Sway Tower 3 miles away. After a short distance the path is level with the original site of Hordle church marked by a cross behind the green fence to the left of the white Hordle House lodge.

Where the Hordle farmland gives way to the Milford-on-Sea cliff top, the path becomes surfaced. Where a now parallel road swings away there is a view ahead down onto Milford promenade with Hurst lighthouse in the distance. To the left on top of the grassy slope is the impressive red-tiled Westover Hall. Continue downhill to pass in front of The White House and reach the Needles Eye Café. Walk up Sea Road behind the café to reach the Milford-on-Sea green.

Historical Notes

Milford-on-Sea has lost its ford but the mill remains as a private house in Barnes Lane. The last miller not only grew and ground his own corn but baked and delivered bread until 1899. The partly Norman church was once served by canons from Christchurch Priory who may have slept beneath the lean-to roofs at the base of the 12th century tower. The squat spire was added in 1827. In the chancel a small stained glass window depicts Charles I with a halo – he was held at nearby Hurst Castle shortly before his execution.

During the 1801 Christmas morning sermon, the congregation saw Newlands Manor in flames through the north windows. One by one villagers left until the vicar paused to ask the verger where everyone had gone. The house belonged to Nelson's colleague Admiral Cornwallis who is commemorated on the church's north wall along with his friend Captain Whitby. The captain's wife Mary Ann, who organised the rebuilding of the mansion and running of the estate, is described as possessing 'masculine sense with every feminine charm'.

In 1815 the Admiral padlocked his pew and started attending Milton church when the curate took advantage of the vicar's almost permanent absence to deliver fiery sermons. One Sunday the incumbent reappeared during morning service to demand use of the pulpit. The curate replied by asking the congregation 'Who is on the Lord's side?' and leading the majority out of the church. Within a year the breakaway group had founded the Baptist church in Barnes Lane but the village remained divided and once sparrows were released in the chapel during an evening service.

On the west side of the old churchyard and to the right of the white kissing gate is the tomb of Charles Dickens' granddaughter Beatrice Byard (the second in the second row). Almost at the far end of the back row is the grave of Sir Edgar Whitehead, the last but one Prime Minister of Southern Rhodesia.

Among the shops around the village green is the unique Grocers' General Store which sells a huge range of branded food products from Canada and the USA. Even American military bases buy from this little shop which operates a large mail order business. It is also noted for its 50 varieties of cheese.

Newlands Manor was a thatched farmhouse when first owned by Admiral William Cornwallis. After being damaged by fire in 1801 it was rebuilt in its present Gothic style under the direction of 19 year old Mary Whitby, wife of Captain Whitby who was away at sea with the Admiral. The work was completed in 1805 and following Captain Whitby's death the following year Mary and her daughter were invited to live here. The Admiral's will directed that his body should be buried in the same church vault as the captain and the property pass to Mrs Whitby. Her grandson later took the name Cornwallis-West and entertained the Prince of Wales (Edward VII), the Kaiser and Lillie Langtry who were all friends of his Irish wife, Mary. The couple's son George shocked society by marrying Winston Churchill's widowed mother whilst the daughters became the Princess of Pless and the Duchess of Westminster. The house is now divided into apartments.

Hordle: There were cliff falls in the early 19th century but in 1830 most villagers were already living away from the sea and it was considered that a more central position would anyway be more convenient. Ten months later the 11th century church had been re-erected here. However, this building had to be replaced by the present red brick structure in 1872. The sanctuary screen from the present building has been made into the gates by Vicarage Lane. A 13th century tombstone from the original site is behind the noticeboard near the lychgate which has the traditional resting place for a coffin. The massive grey monument beyond the church's east end commemorates John Collet (1798–1856) who was known as the 'Poachers' Friend' because he often paid their fines.

On the north-east corner of the church a tiny modern plaque records the burial in 1886 in an unmarked grave of the English Shaker leader Mary Girling. She claimed to be the incarnation of Christ and arrived from Battersea in 1872 with 12 disciples who believed she would never die. This 'Children of God Community' was at Hordle Grange on the road to Tiptoe until evicted for failing to pay rent just before Christmas 1874. Auberon Herbert, a vegetarian who was famous for dining with his servants and encouraging farm workers to form a union, offered accommodation in his barn at Ashley Arnewood, 1 mile to the west, and continued to employ two Shakers after Mrs Girling's death.

Yeatton House: A rockery in the garden is formed largely from Hordle's ancient church. The walled kitchen garden is now Apple Court nursery where visitors are welcome.

Hooper's Hill: This short narrow road, stopped up at the north end, was once the main road as the markings and 'cats eyes' suggest. At the junction with Angel Lane there is a white milestone in the bushes indicating Christchurch 7 Lymington 5.

Angel Lane is named after a 19th century family. The New Milton water tower which is seen from here was built in 1900 to look like a fort and stands near the station. Ashley Clinton to the south, with its own water tower, was the home of General Sir Henry Clinton who fought at the Battle of Waterloo. The family remained until Miss Clinton's death in 1956 when their collection of military uniforms was presented to the National Army Museum.

Becton Bunny is a small valley carrying a stream to the sea. (See page 85 for 'bunny' explanation). This bunny is still in its natural state with plenty of pink thrift in summer and the stream running onto the beach rather than piped. The surrounding land is now part of Barton-on-Sea golf club which has recently extended its course onto Becton Farm having lost around 15 acres in 20 years through cliff falls. For over 50 years the farm was the home of the Coakes family including Marion Mould who as Miss Coakes rode her famous horse Stroller here.

Taddiford Gap: 'Táddi' means 'toad' and this valley path, once used by smugglers, is now defended by two concrete dragon's teeth left over from a continuous line across the landing point thought to be favoured by the Germans in 1940.

Sway Tower was built between 1879 and 1885 for former Calcutta judge Andrew Peterson to provide employment. Peterson, who became a clairvoyant after meeting the Shakers in Hordle, claimed to be guided by both the 16th century Italian sculptor Cellini and Sir Christopher Wren. Revolutionary concrete blocks were used for the Indian style building with shingle for the cement being brought up from Milford beach. The tower was built from inside without the need for scaffolding. Trinity

House refused to allow a light to be placed on top of the 218 ft structure in case ships mistook it for a lighthouse. The folly, now known as simply Sway Tower, became a hotel in 1991.

Hordle House dates from the 18th century when the village was still here rather than inland. The present Hordle church was largely paid for by J.P. Kennard who was living here in the 1870s. Later the house was home of Lord Justice Thesiger who died suddenly in 1880 at the early age of 42 as a result of too much swimming in the sea. The house has been a school since 1926 when the first pupils included the Duke of St Albans, the Hereditary Grand Falconer of England, and Anthony Harris, son of 'Bomber' Harris. Another past pupil is film director Derek Jarman. Until the 1940 invasion scare Hordle House still had its own wooden steps down to the beach. Just west of the lodge is the old churchyard where a cross marks the position of the dismantled church. Among those thought to be buried here are Sir Reginald de Clerk who died in the Wars of the Roses and Christopher Clark who died in 1720 aged 112. Many other tombs contain shipwrecked sailors. In the winter of 1818 there were 9 bodies in the church awaiting burial after the *True Blue Tar* was wrecked in the bay on her way home from Sierra Leone. An earlier entry in the register reads: 'Woman, unknown, aged 20 to 24 found on Hordle shore 13 Augst. – naked except for her stockings, with gold ring, and apparently a nurse, with bruises on breast and head. Coroner's verdict – 'Found drown'd nothing further being discoverable' buried Aug. 15th 1809.' The old church was used as a trig point by the Ordnance Survey before the present familiar column was placed in the field to the southwest. At the end of August an annual service is held on the site of the old church when the choir takes its place in the chancel whilst other villagers sit in the outline of the nave.

Westover Hall, built in 1897 for the Siemens family of electricity fame, has been described as a 'flamboyant piece of late Victoriana'. The architect was Arnold Mitchell and inside there are tiles by William de Morgan and stained glass. The

94

house, later home of Oxford car manufacturer William Morris, who as Lord Nuffield founded Nuffield College, is now a hotel noted for its food.

The White House was built in 1903 as a seaside residence for the Walker Munro family of Rhinefield House in the New Forest. The architect was Romaine Walker who had just undertaken his greatest work, Danesfield in Buckinghamshire for Robert Hudson of soap fame. This seaside house is in the shape of a U enclosing a terraced courtyard facing the sea. The 'Arts and Crafts' style incorporates a 'lighthouse' feature and a 'bridge' over the main entrance. After being owned by the health authority the future of this now empty building is uncertain but planning permission exists for conversion to flats.

Bibliography

Ashley, Harry *The Dorset Coast* (Countryside Books 1992)
Ashley, Harry *The Dorset Village Book* (Countryside Books 1984)
Bond, Lillian *Tyneham, a Lost Heritage* (Dovecote Press 1956)
Hatts, Leigh *The Bournemouth Coast Path* (Countryside Books 1985)
Jesty, Chris *A Guide to the Isle of Purbeck* (Dovecote Press 1984)
Legg, Rodney *Guide to Purbeck Coast and Shipwreck* (Dorset Publishing Co. 1984)
Legg, Rodney *Old Swanage* (Dorset Publishing Co. 1983)
Lloyd, A.T. *New Milton in Old Postcards* (European Library 1985)
New, Anthony *A Guide to the Abbeys of England and Wales* (Constable 1985)
Newman, John and Pevsner, Nikolaus *Buildings of England: Dorset* (Penguin 1972)
Parris, Leslie *Constable: Paintings, Watercolours and Drawings* (Tate 1976)
Dorset Federation of Women's Institutes *Hidden Dorset* (Countryside Books 1990)